Teashop Walks
in SUSSEX

The view along the Seven Sisters cliffs toward Beachy Head is one of the finest in Sussex.

Rupert Matthews

S.B. Publications

First published in 2007 by S. B. Publications
Tel: 01323 893498
Email: sbpublications@tiscali.co.uk
www.sbpublications.co.uk

ISBN 978-185770-331-3

Designed and Typeset by EH Graphics (01273) 515527

Front cover photo: Open field leading down to Jevington village.
Back cover photo: Stile beside a metal gate, Wisborough Green.

Contents

Teashop Walks in Sussex

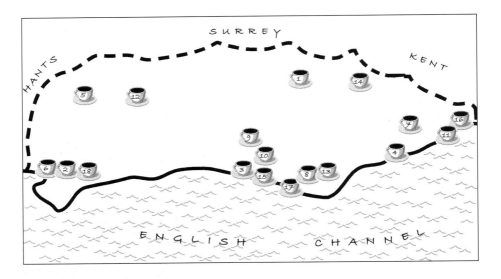

Shorter Walks

1 Wych Cross
2 Chichester
3 Brighton
4 Bexhill
5 Midhurst
6 Fishbourne

Middle Distance Walks

7 Battle
8 Alfriston
9 Ditchling

10 Stanmer
11 Winchelsea
12 Wisborough Green
13 Jevington

Longer Walks

14 Northiam
15 Rottingdean
16 Rye
17 Seaford
18 Tangmere

Introduction

"Afternoon tea is the finest contribution that England has made to cuisine", or so my grandmother always had it. And she was in a position to know. My childhood memories are filled with images of that kindly lady cutting Victoria sponges, handing round buttered scones and pouring out cups of nice fresh tea.

Ever since those long off days I have had a particular affinity for afternoon tea. I like to keep a cake on the go at home so that, come 4 o'clock, I can cut off a slice and take a break from the work of writing to sip a hot cup of tea and munch on the cake. I'm sure my wife thinks I'm a bit odd.

Essential as a cuppa and a cake at the desk might be to the working day, it cannot possibly compare with a visit to a traditional tea shop. I might have a cake at home, but a good tea shop will have a whole range of cakes from which slices can be carved as well as a range of buns, pastries and scones. And if you are lucky there will be cucumber sandwiches on offer as well. There is nothing quite like a good tea shop. I confess that I am totally unable to see one without wanting to pop in.

The delicious cream tea served in the Jevington Tea Gardens, see Walk 13.

Addicted as I might be to the delights of a cream tea, I know full well that the tasty dainties can add worryingly to the waistline. So all visits to a teashop should be accompanied by a bit of light exercise - a walk.

Such is the purpose of this book.

I have selected 18 of the finest tea shops that Sussex has to offer and that lie close to a convenient walk that offers something by way of scenery, history, wildlife or art. I hope that you enjoy the walks and the teas. I have certainly enjoyed putting this book together and would like to thank the many local residents who have helped me with the task.

Walk No. 1   Wych Cross

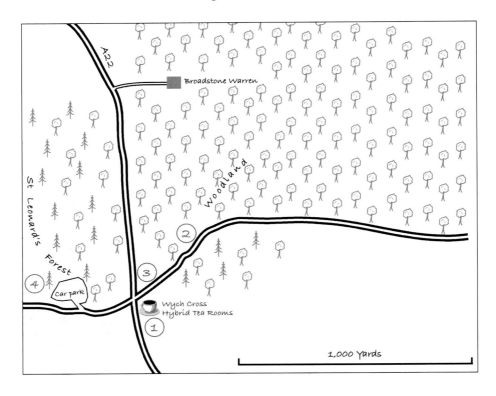

1 Wych Cross

Distance:	**1 to 3 miles**
Route:	**Wych Cross - St Leonard's Forest - Wych Cross**
Map:	**OS Explorer 135**
Teashop:	**Hybrid Tea Rooms, Wych Cross Nurseries.**
Open:	**Monday to Saturday 9.30 - 4.30**
Parking:	**There is a car park at Wych Cross Nurseries.**
Public Transport:	**Wych Cross is served by the Metrobus Bus route 291 from East Grinstead.**
Conditions:	**This walk is through the National Trust woodland that spreads out across the hills north of Wych Cross towards Broadstone Warren. There is no set route as the walker is free to choose their own path through these extensive forests.**

As woodland walks go, this cannot be bettered. St Leonard's Forest is an expanse of woodland that stretches across northern Sussex. Although it is in places patchy and discontinuous St Leonard's Forest is a charming and relatively wild area of the county. Bridleways, paths and tracks wind their way through the trees offering a range of routes and vistas to be enjoyed.

The Walk

1) Find your way to Wych Cross Nurseries.

The tea rooms here have led the way in the modern trend for garden centres to have excellent places to eat. Indeed, many locals come here more to take tea than to browse the roses and other plants - excellent though they are. The restaurant is named the Hybrid Tea Room in honour of the hybrid tea roses in which Wych Cross Nurseries specialise. The cakes are all home-made by the staff and the tea is served piping hot.

2) Leave the Nurseries and turn right at the exit from the car park. Walk along the grass verge of the lane.

The land to your left is an extensive area of fairly dense woodland that is criss-crossed by bridleways and footpaths. If this sort of heavy forest cover is not to your taste there is some more open countryside to explore.

3) On leaving the Nurseries car park turn left. Cross the main A22 and continue straight on for about 200 yards down a lane to find a gravel car park on your right. This car park opens out onto wooded heathlands and gorse country that stretches for miles.

This is St Leonard's Forest that spreads across northern Sussex right from Horsham across to Crawley and south to Handcross. It covers about 12 square miles in area and rises to a height of about 280 feet above sea level, though the rolling ground has no obvious hills. In Roman times this was just part of the vast Andereswald woodlands that blanketed the Weald for over a hundred miles east to west.

By the time of King John in the 13th century St Leonard's Forest had been acquired by the monarch for use as a hunting forest. The entire area was never either forested or bereft of people, these medieval hunting grounds were interspersed with farms and the woodlands were managed to produce timber and game. The folk who lived there had rights, but also responsibilities, not shared by others.

The sign that indicates the entrance to the Garden Centre at Wych Cross.

As late as 1794 the Forest was described as "an extensive tract of waste land producing nothing but rabbits". William Cobbett's verdict in 1823 was no better; "I have seldom travelled over 8 miles so well calculated to fill the mind with painful reflections. The soil is poor, miserable, clayey-looking sand, with a sort of sandstone underneath". Nowadays, it is no longer a giant forest but a patchwork of woodlands and heath, interspersed with areas of farmland. It is intersected by a series of streams, or gills as they are known locally. The county council has recently made efforts to open the woodland and heaths up for walkers, and you are generally welcome to wander as you wish.

St. Leonard's Forest is named in honour of a French saint of that name who came to Sussex in the violent days when the Kingdom of Sussex was ruled by pagan English kings. The history of those Dark Ages is rather obscure and precise dates are difficult to come by, but St Leonard's visit probably took place around the year 540.

Whenever he came, St Leonard did not enjoy his visit. The singing nightingales kept him awake as he slept on the forest floor, and he was bitten by a snake - presumably an adder. White lilies are said to have sprung up where the saint's holy blood fell from the wound. Despite this St Leonard's trip was a great success and he managed to convert the local

English to Christianity. God was delighted and asked St Leonard what he wanted by way of thanks. The holy Frenchman asked that the snakes of the forest be struck deaf, which seems fair enough, and then went on to demand that the nightingales be struck dumb, which seems a little harsh. Even today no nightingales sing in St Leonard's Forest.

Some centuries later an altogether larger and more powerful serpent appeared in St Leonard's Forest. This was a true dragon and the contemporary account from 1614 leaves little to the imagination. The spelling and grammar are as in the original.

"TRUE AND WONDERFUL"

"A Discourse relating a strange and monstrous Serpent (or Dragon) lately discovered, and yet living, to the great Annoyance and divers Slaughters both of Men and Cattell, by his strong and violent Poyson. In Sussex, two miles from Horsam, in a Woode called St. Leonards Forrest, and thirtie miles from London, this present month of August, 1614. With the true Generation of Serpents.

"In Sussex, there is a pretty market-towne, called Horsam, neare unto it a forrest, called St. Leonard's Forrest, and there, in a vast and unfrequented place, heathie, vaultie, full of unwholesome shades, and over-growne hollowes, where this serpent is thought to be bred; but, wheresoever bred, certaine and too true it is, that there it yet lives. Within three or four miles compasse, are its usual haunts, oftentimes at a place called Faygate, and it hath been seen within halfe a mile of Horsam; a wonder, no doubt, most terrible and noisome to the inhabitants thereabouts. There is always in his tracke or path left a glutinous and slimie matter (as by a small similitude we may perceive in a snaile's) which is very corrupt and offensive to the scent; insomuch that they perceive the air to be putrified withall, which must needes be very dangerous. For though the corruption of it cannot strike the outward part of a man, unless heated into his blood; yet by receiving it in at any of our breathing organs (the mouth or nose) it is by authoritie of all authors, writing in that kinde, mortall and deadlie, as one thus saith :

"'Noxia serpentum est admixto sanguine pestis. - LUCAN'

"This serpent (or dragon, as some call it) is reputed to be nine feete, or rather more, in length, and shaped almost in the forme of an axeltree of a cart; a quantitie of thickness in the middest, and somewhat smaller at both endes. The former part, which he shootes forth as a necke, is supposed to be an elle long; with a white ring, as it were, of scales about it. The scales along his backe seem to be blackish, and so much as is discovered under his bellie, appeareth to be red; for I speak of no nearer description than of a reasonable ocular distance. For coming too neare it, hath already beene too dearly payd for, as you shall heare hereafter.

"It is likewise discovered to have large feete, but the eye may be there deceived; for some suppose that serpents have no feete, but glide upon certain ribbes and scales, which both defend them from the upper part of their throat unto the lower part of their bellie, and also cause them to move much the faster. For so this doth, and rids way (as we call it) as fast as a man can run. He is of Countenance very proud, and at the sight of men or cattel, will raise his necke upright, and seem to listen and looke about, with great arrogancy. There

The open woodland of St Leonard's Forest offers many enjoyable routes for walking in this section of the Sussex Weald.

are likewise on either side of him discovered, two great bunches so big as a large foote-ball and (as some thinke) will in time grow to wings; but God, I hope, will (to defend the poor people in the neighbourhood) that he shall be destroyed before he grow so fledge.

"He will cast his venome about four rodde from him, as by woefull experience it was proved on the bodies of a man and a woman comming that way, who afterwards were found dead, being poysoned and very much swelled, but not prayed upon. Likewise a man going to chase it, and as he imagined, to destroy it with two mastive dogs, as yet not knowing the great danger of it, his dogs were both killed, and he himselfe glad to returne with hast to preserve his own life. Yet this is to be noted, that the dogs were not prayed upon, but slaine and left whole : for his is thought to be, for the most part, in a conie-warren, which he much frequents; and it is found much scanted and impaired in the encrease it had woont to afford.

"These persons, whose names are hereunder printed, have seene this serpent, beside divers others, as the carrier of Horsam, who lieth at the White Horse in Southwarke, and who can certifie the truth of all that has been here related".

(signed) "John Steele, Christopher Holder, And a Widow Woman dwelling nere Faygate"

4) *Having braved the risk of sudden death from the venom of a hideous dragon, if it still lives, which hopefully it does not, you should retrace your steps to the Wych Cross Nurseries.*

Walk No. 2 — Chichester

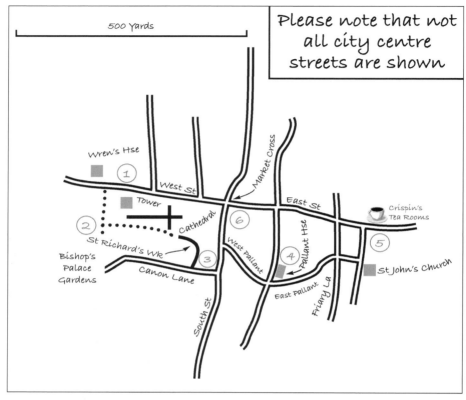

500 Yards

Please note that not all city centre streets are shown

Wren's Hse
1
West St
Market Cross
Tower
East St
2
Cathedral
St Richard's Wk
West Pallant
6
Pallant Hse
Crispin's Tea Rooms
Bishop's Palace Gardens
Canon Lane
3
4
5
St John's Church
South St
East Pallant
Friary La

There is some controversy as to whether Wren's House was actually designed by Sir Christopher Wren or merely by a skilled imitator of his work.

2 Chichester

Distance:	**1 mile**
Route:	**Chichester**
Map:	**OS Explorer 120**
Teashop:	**Crispin's, East St, Chichester.**
Open:	**Monday to Saturday 9 - 4.30**
Parking:	**There are several car parks in Chichester.**
Public Transport:	**Tangmere is served by main line railway and several bus routes.**
Conditions:	**This walk is entirely over city centre paths and pavements. There are no steep hills.**

This city centre stroll passes all the key sites of this beautiful city. The mighty cathedral, Market Cross and St Mary's Hospital are the main medieval features of a city that is overwhelmingly Georgian in character. This is a bustling centre so be prepared to encounter crowds of shoppers and tourists as well as architectural wonder. The city is the oldest in the county, having been built by the Romans on the site of a British settlement of some kind. Known as Noviomagus, it formed an important port for southern Britain throughout the Roman times.

When the English invaded the new king, Aelle, gave the city to his son Cissa. The old English term for a fortified Roman site was "chester", so the city became known as "Cissa's Chester" and so Chichester. The early English kept the Roman street plan, though they gave the main streets the very English names of West Street, East Street, South Street and North Street

The towering spire of Chichester Cathedral has dominated the city for centuries and makes an easily identifiable point from which to start the walk.

which they retain to this day. There is nothing left above ground to testify to the Roman and early English days of Chichester, though the City Museum has some fine artefacts to show. The city to be seen today is mainly Georgian in character with some medieval survivals.

The Walk

1) Find your way to the cathedral in West Street. From there walk west to find Wren's House - a fine Stuart mansion reputedly designed by Sir Christopher Wren - on your right, then

Chichester is unique among English cathedrals in having a separate bell tower, something more common on the Continent than in England.

return to the West Front of the Cathedral.

The cathedral is the most striking building in Chichester. The cathedral was begun in 1091 by Bishop Ralph Luffa after the seat of the diocese was moved from Selsey. The most noticeable feature is the bell tower, unique among English cathedrals in that it is separate from the main body of the building. It was erected in around 1390 and refaced in the mid-20th century. The tower is occasionally open and can be climbed, but the stairs are narrow and steep. Most people prefer to visit the Cathedral.

The cathedral is essentially that built by Bishop Ralph, though part of it burned down in 1187 and the tower collapsed in 1861. Both times the rebuilding was carried out skilfully and with sympathy. There is much to see inside this splendid cathedral and a visit makes a wonderful addition to this walk. Enter by way of the West Door and leave the same way.

Just outside the West Door is a magnificent modern statue of St Richard, the patron saint of both Chichester and coachdrivers. Richard de Wych was born in 1197 and, as the second son, was sent to join the Church by his parents. The boy acquired a reputation for learning and theological knowledge, but had to leave the church when his brother died and his nephew was too young to look after the family estates. The guardian appointed by Richard's brother turned out to be a dishonest man who stripped the estates of their wealth. Richard moved in, ousted the guardian and spent years managing the family lands before turning them over to his nephew and returning to the Church. The years spent on the estates made Richard skilled at business and farming, as well as the more usual sacred skills of a churchman.

The statue of St Richard, patron saint of Chichester, that stands outside the Cathedral's West Door.

When he was elected Bishop of Chichester in 1245 Richard put both sets of skills to good use. He restored the secular fortunes of the diocese and boosted its reputation for learning and for education. Once, when celebrating mass in the cathedral he dropped the chalice holding the sacred wine. The chalice fell to the floor, but landed without a drop being spilled, a fact generally accounted a miracle. Richard was made a saint after he died and is usually shown with a chalice at his feet.

2) From the statue of St Richard continue south for a few yards, then turn left to enter the cloisters. These were built in around 1400 and have a roof of Irish oak. Walk the length of the cloisters to exit at the southeastern corner into a narrow stone-flagged

The walk leaves the Cathedral cloisters by way of this narrow and initially uninviting lane, St Richard's Walk.

footpath known as St. Richard's Walk. Follow this walk as it bends to the right past some almshouses to emerge into Canon Lane.

As its name suggests, this lane was built to house the clergy from the cathedral. The area was destroyed in the fire of 1187 and rebuilt. Several of the houses date back to this rebuilding though they have been much altered over the years. If you turn west along Canon Lane you will reach the entrance to the Bishop's Palace Gardens, which are open to the public when they are not being used for Church functions. The main walk, however, goes in the opposite direction.

3) Turn east along Canon Lane to walk through the medieval Canon's Arch into South Street. The Tourist Information Office is to the right. Turn left up South Street, then take the first right, West Pallant. At the far end of West Pallant is found Pallant House, now an art gallery.

The Pallant area of Chichester was for many years the most fashionable part of the city. During the Georgian period the wealthy Sussex families vied to build the best and most lavish town houses around here. Most of these are still private houses, though their exteriors can be enjoyed by anyone who walks past.

Pallant House was, and remains, the finest town house of all in Chichester. It is now an art gallery that has the finest collection of modern British art outside the Tate Gallery in London. Much of this

Pallant House is home to a gallery of modern art that has won several awards.

collection is housed in an award-winning extension to the north of the old house, but Pallant House itself also houses artworks. Whether you are interested in the art or the building the place is worth a visit and Chichester is rightly proud of the gallery. Pallant House also features a café that serves afternoon tea.

The Pallant area of the city is famed for its elegant Georgian town houses.

4) Leaving Pallant House continue east along East Pallant to cross Friary Lane and so reach

A row of ancient cottages in East Pallant marks the edge of the Georgian area of Chichester.

St John's Street. The street is named for the charming St John's Church, which is usually open. Turn left to walk north along St John's Street. This meets East Street at a T-junction. In front of you and slightly to the right is Crispin's Tea Shop.

The facade of Crispin's is unprepossessing, but behind it lurks a gem of a tea shop. What was the front room of the fine Georgian house in which it is located is taken up with the counter in which is displayed an astonishingly varied selection of home-made cakes, scones, biscuits and buns - all made on the premises. The handmade eccles cakes are a particular speciality and nobody should call here without trying one. The tea rooms are open for lunch as well as morning coffee and afternoon tea, serving a variety of sandwiches, quiches and other light meals, again made here.

Crispin's Tea Rooms lie inside a town house in Chichester's East Street.

Beyond the front room is a genteel parlour retaining much of the original period fixtures. Beyond that is another large room for those taking tea and, in the summer months, the back yard is opened up as a patio. Everything here is civilised and homely, having been run by the same family for the past 20 years. The owner has got the serving of a delicious cream tea down to a fine art.

5) Having taken tea, leave Crispin's and turn right to walk west along East Street. The massive portico of the Corn Market towers up on the left. After a few yards the street becomes pedestrianised. Continue straight on to reach the Market Cross where West Street, East Street, North Street and South Street all meet.

The beautiful Market Cross was erected in 1500 by the then Bishop of Chichester, Edward Story and is sometimes called Story's Cross. It stands over 50 feet tall and is made of the hard white stone from Caen in Normandy. It takes the form of an

The patio area of Crispin's is lovely in warm sunny weather.

octagonal arcade centered around a massive central pillar from which spring flying buttresses that are topped by a stone cupola. The structure has been altered slightly over the years, most famously by having a bust of King Charles I installed to replace a saint after that king's execution. The general design is, however, pretty much as Bishop Story intended it.

In former times the main market of Chichester took place in this square, with stalls sheltering under the arches of the Market Cross in inclement

Eccles cakes are a speciality at Crispin's. Like all other baked treats served here they are produced on the premises.

weather. These days the market is gone, but the cross is still much loved by the folk of Chichester who sit here to chat or rest while out shopping in the city centre.

6) From the Market Cross continue west into West Street to return to the start of the walk.

The medieval Market Cross dominates the crossroads that has been the centre of life in Chichester for at least 1,900 years.

Walk No. 3 — Brighton

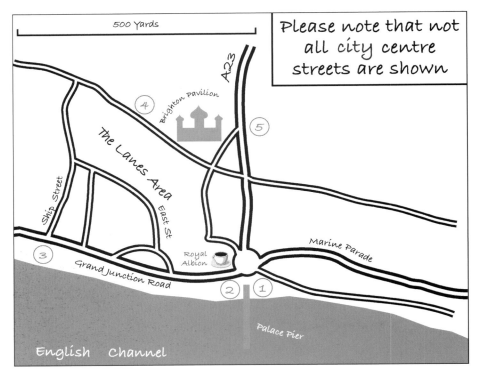

500 Yards

Please note that not all city centre streets are shown

A23

Brighton Pavilion

④

⑤

The Lanes Area

Ship Street

East St

Marine Parade

Royal Albion

③

Grand Junction Road

② ①

Palace Pier

English Channel

Brighton's Palace Pier is now the only one of the three Victorian originals to still be standing. It is open year round free of charge.

3 Brighton

Distance:	**1 mile**
Route:	**Brighton**
Map:	**OS Explorer 122**
Teashop:	**Royal Albion Hotel, Grand Junction Road, Brighton.**
Parking:	**There are car parks in Brighton.**
Public Transport:	**Brighton is served by mainline railway.**
Conditions:	**This walk is entirely over city centre pavements with no difficult terrain.**

Brighton was a sleepy fishing village until it was discovered by the Prince Regent, later King George IV, in 1783. Thereafter the place swiftly became a focus for fashionable Society as "Prinny" and his pals flocked to the seaside for bathing, dining, gambling and drinking. They demanded suitable housing in which to stay and leisure facilities, transforming the village into a town dedicated to pleasure. The arrival of the railway in Victorian times transformed the town again allowing vast crowds of daytrippers and weekenders from London to flood into Brighton by the thousand. This walk takes in the key central sights of this holiday town.

The Walk

1) Find your way to the Palace Pier.

This was one of those grand Victorian piers that epitomised the British seaside resort for generations of holiday makers. In its heyday Palace Pier boasted all the usual seaside delights, and many of them survive to this day. The helter-skelter is a particular favourite with children, but there are also dodgems, a big wheel and vast numbers of slot machines. Entrance to Palace Pier is now free and it is recommended that any visitor to Brighton should take a stroll out to the end and back - though the choice of candyfloss, ice cream or popcorn is down to personal preference.

Brighton originally had three piers. The Chain Pier came down in a storm in 1896. The West Pier survived rather longer. It fell into disuse in the later 20th century and became derelict. There were various schemes to restore it, including turning it into private housing, but while the authorities debated and prevaricated disaster struck. The old structure caught fire and was destroyed in a furnace of flames. Only the shattered metal uprights remain of what was one of the grandest piers on the South Coast.

2) Leaving Palace Pier, turn left to walk west along the Promenade.

This is the original Victorian Promenade that backs the shingle beach for which Brighton is

The Lanes area of Brighton is full of small squares, narrow streets and old houses.

so famous. It is this stretch of beach that has long been responsible for Brighton's prosperity. For most of the past two millennia fishing boats were hauled up here when not at sea. The little fishing village of Brighthelmstone had a population in the hundreds, most of them earning a living from the sea one way or another.

Then, in 1754, Dr Richard Russell came here from Lewes. He believed that sea air, sea bathing and sea water were essential to good health, so any of his patients who seemed generally unwell was prescribed a trip to Brighton with vigorous swimming and walking included. People being what they are, Dr Russell's patients were not content with swimming and walking - they needed food, drink and entertainment as well. A bustling little collection of businesses sprang up to cater for the patients of Dr Russell and the other Sussex doctors who followed his lead.

In 1783 Prince George, later to be Prince Regent and later still King George IV, came to Brighton. His Highness had little time for swimming or walking, but was famously addicted to food, drink and entertainment. He loved the place and Brighton's fame was assured.

Brighton Pavilion is a riot of exotic eastern architecture wrapped around a Georgian country house.

3) After about 400 yards turn right into Ship Street beside the Ship Hotel. The area to the east of Ship Street is known as The Lanes.

This is what remains of the fishing village of Brighthelmstone. It was burnt down by the French twice in the 16th century so little remains of the medieval original, but the houses, shops and pubs that crowd together are a charming mixture of Stuart and Georgian constructions. The Lanes are most famous for their antique and curio shops, but there are fashion shops and restaurants as well. Probably the oldest remaining feature of old Brighton is the font inside St Nicholas Church. The church itself is a Victorian rebuilding of a 14th century original, but the font is over 900 years old.

After exploring The Lanes, exit to the north to reach Western Road, which runs parallel to the Promenade. This marked the northern edge of the village in the 1780s, so when Prince George wanted to build a seaside holiday home he chose to build it just north of this road. And what a holiday home it turned out to be.

4) Turn right along Western Road. Just before the junction with the A23 London Road, Prince George's Brighton Pavilion looms up on the left.

The Pavilion was begun in 1787 as a fairly standard late Georgian country house - though several rooms were completed in the Chinese style that was then fashionable. Prince George - widely known as "Prinny" - loved the place and spent increasingly long periods of time here. It was conveniently close to the court in London, but far enough away that Prinny could enjoy himself without being pestered by tedious government business.

The gardens behind the Pavilion are open to the public and can be enjoyed by any passerby.

In 1815 Prinny decided that his home in Brighton was neither big enough, grand enough nor bizarre enough. He called in the architect John Nash and told him to extend and remodel the house in the style of the Indian Mughal Emperors. Nash went to work with a will, adding onion domes, minarets and pinnacles in an orgy of fantasy architecture. The result was everything that Prinny could have desired for a holiday home and when it was finished in 1822 he moved in almost permanently. His brother and successor, King William IV, also loved the place and used it regularly.

Despite her straight-laced image acquired in later years, Prinny's niece Queen Victoria also loved Brighton and spent many happy holidays here in her youth. But by 1845 Brighton had grown to such an extent that the Pavilion became surrounded by other people's houses. The place no longer offered a remote hiding place for royalty, so Victoria abandoned it. The Pavilion was later bought by the council and is now open to the public. The interior is as fantastical as the exterior and well worth a visit.

5) On leaving the Brighton Pavilion, turn south along the A23 London Road toward the seafront and Palace Pier. Immediately before reaching the pier, the Royal Albion Hotel stands on the right.

There are, of course, more places to drink a cup of tea in Brighton than anywhere else in Sussex. This walk passes at least 20 of them, but for sheer position and gentility none can quite match the Royal Albion Hotel. The lounge of the hotel, in which afternoon tea is served, has enormous plate glass picture windows in a great curve overlooking the sea, Promenade and the Pier. On a fine day you can sit here and watch the crowds of holiday-makers and daytrippers surging along the sea front. On grimmer days you can sit here and watch the stormy seas crashing their surf onto the beach while rain lashes the pavements, and you are in the warmth and comfort of the hotel.

Nor are the attractions limited to the views and comfortable seating. The Royal Albion serves its afternoon tea in fine china and offers a wide variety of delicious cakes, pastries and sandwiches. Grand and genteel this most certainly is.

Brighton's Royal Albion Hotel offers a splendid afternoon tea overlooking the seafront.

Brighton Pavilion was built as a seaside retreat for the Prince Regent, later King George IV. His statue stands outside the building.

Walk No. 4 — Bexhill

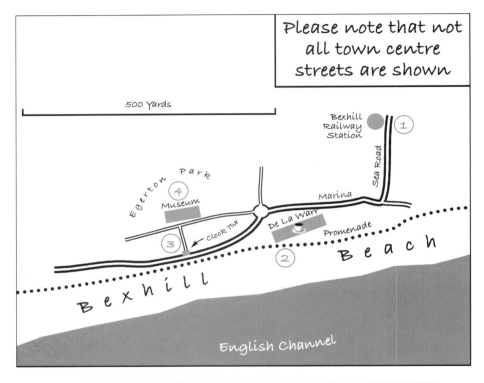

Please note that not all town centre streets are shown

500 Yards

Bexhill Railway Station

Sea Road

Egerton Park

4 Museum

Marina

De La Warr

Clock Twr

Promenade

3

2

English Channel

Bexhill Beach

The 1930s masterpiece of restrained modernist architecture is the De La Warr Pavilion that dominates the seafront at Bexhill.

4 Bexhill

Distance:	**Up to 2 miles**
Route:	**Bexhill**
Map:	**OS Explorer 124**
Teashop:	**De La Warr Pavilion, Bexhill-on-Sea.**
Parking:	**There are car parks and on-street parking in Bexhill.**
Public Transport:	**Bexhill is served by frequent railway services. The walk starts and ends at the railway station.**
Conditions:	**This walk is entirely over town centre pavements with no steep hills or difficult terrain.**

This bracing seaside walk takes in the promenade of Bexhill with its views over the extensive sandy beaches that made this town such a popular seaside resort. The walk passes some noted 1930's architectural gems as well as the usual seaside staples of ice cream stands, crazy-golf, candy floss and pubs.

The Walk

1) Find your way to Bexhill Railway Station. On leaving turn right down Sea Road, which is lined with shops, candyfloss stalls and amusement arcades as one might expect from a seaside resort. At the far end of Sea Road cross over the Marina road to find the seafront footpath of the Promenade. Turn right to walk along the beach. As you approach the

dominating white mass of the De La Warr Pavilion, turn off the Promenade to enter this most impressive building.

The De La Warr Pavilion is an acknowledged masterpiece of 1930's architecture. It was constructed in 1935 by the Bauhaus partnership of Erich Mendelsohn and Serge Chermayeff. This was one of their first joint ventures and perhaps the most successful. Chermayeff had been born in Russia, but moved to England when still a boy. After leaving school he took up interior design as a career and was responsible for the inside of the BBC's Broadcasting House

Beach huts on the shingle section of beach at Bexhill. These huts are in high demand during the summer months.

Bexhill boasts two crazy-golf courses, both on the route of the walk. This is the seafront course on the Promenade.

before designing a range of furniture and upholstery fabrics.

At the time of the De La Warr Pavilion, it was Erich Mendelsohn who was the more accomplished architect. He was thirteen years older than Chermayeff and had designed several important buildings in his native Germany before he fled the Nazi regime in 1933 and came to Britain. He specialised in factories, so the De La Warr Pavilion was as much a new venture for him as for Chermayeff. The two men worked well together, jointly sharing the credit for both the architecture and interior design. They went on to design houses and shops.

In 1940, when it looked as if the Germans might invade and conquer Britain, Chermayeff and Mendelsohn fled once again, this time to the USA. Mendelsohn continued to work as an architect, though he now specialised in synagogues and hospitals. Chermayeff became Professor of Architecture first at Harvard and later at Yale.

If the Germans had invaded, Bexhill would have been one of their key landing beaches. During those grim months the beach was mined and festooned with barbed wire, while the

All the usual seaside treats can be found on the Promenade at Bexhill, including mechanical rides for children, ice creams and toys.

Bexhill's seafront clock tower was erected to commemorate the coronation of King Edward VII at the start of the 20th century.

De La Warr Pavilion was turned over to military use. After the war, the Pavilion was returned to the holiday use for which it was designed. Sadly, Bexhill shared in the general decline of British seaside resorts during the 1980s and by the 1990s was in some disrepair.

It has now recently undergone a massive £9 million refurbishment and is back to its former glory. There is a theatre that can hold over a thousand people plus two art galleries that attract exhibitions by leading British and international contemporary artists. The forecourt has been converted to be an outside auditorium for summer shows. Many people hold that the main attraction remains the building itself with its graceful, sweeping lines and uncompromising bauhaus design.

Be that as it may, of rather more immediate interest may be the restaurant on the top floor. The staff here pride themselves on serving finely cooked fresh, local produce. In the afternoon this means a selection of imaginative cakes as well as the more usual scones and teacakes - all of which are cooked on the premises. Morning coffee is also served.

2) Having enjoyed the delights of the De La Warr Pavilion, return to the Promenade and turn right.

This fine seaside walk extends for over a mile to the west. It is a highly enjoyable walk which offers views out to sea as well as as much fresh air as anyone could want. There are the usual seaside attractions of crazy-golf, ice cream stalls, candy floss and mechanical rides to keep everyone entertained.

3) You can walk as far along the Promenade as you wish, then return to the Clock Tower that stands on an island in West Parade. Head inland here to reach Bexhill Museum and Egerton Park that lies behind it.

The Museum hosts a wide range of local displays, including some fine dinosaur fossils dug up nearby. The Museum is closed on Mondays. The park has extensive gardens, but also tennis courts, bowling greens and a putting green golf course. During the Napoleonic Wars this was a major camping ground for the regiments that guarded the South Coast. The garrisons that manned the Royal Military Canal (See Walk 11 Winchelsea) came from here.

4) Leaving the Museum turn left to walk east along Egerton Road. This meets the Marina road at a mini-roundabout. Go straight ahead to pass the De La Warr Pavilion on its landward side. Continue along the Marina road to the junction with Sea Road. Turn left to return to the railway station where the walk began.

Bexhill's town museum has exhibits from a wide span of the town's story, and even boasts some dinosaur fossils.

Walk No. 5 — Midhurst

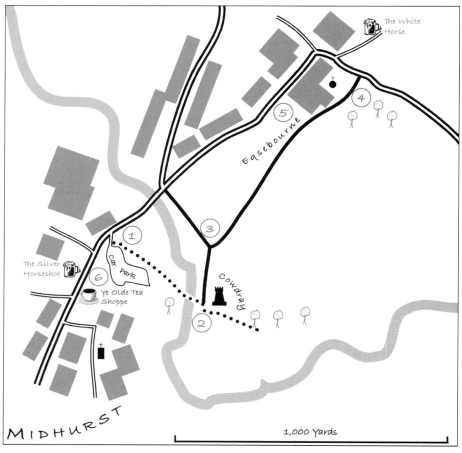

The Silver Horseshoe

Ye Olde Tea Shoppe

Car Park

The White Horse

Easebourne

Cowdray

MIDHURST

1,000 Yards

The path from Midhurst to Cowdray crosses the River Rother by way of this ancient bridge.

5 Midhurst

Distance:	**2 miles**
Route:	**Midhurst - Cowdray - Easebourne - Midhurst**
Map:	**OS Explorer 133**
Teashop:	**Ye Olde Tea Shoppe, North St, Midhurst**
Open:	**10 - 5.30 daily**
Parking:	**There is a car park and limited on-street parking in Midhurst.**
Public Transport:	**Midhurst is served by Stagecoach bus route 60 from Chichester.**
Conditions:	**This walk is partly over open fields and partly along surfaced roadside pavements. There are no difficult slopes or surfaces.**

There is much of interest packed into this short walk. Cowdray Castle was once one of the foremost strongholds of Sussex and then a magnificent mansion before centuries of neglect took their toll. The ruins are still of interest, while the church at Easebourne was once a priory and has a charm all its own.

The Walk

1) Find your way to the car park at the northern end of Midhurst which has the Tourist Information Office in a small building on its western side. Opposite the Tourist Information Office a footpath leaves the car park near its entrance through a gate to strike off arrow-straight along a causeway raised above marshy meadows. Follow this causeway towards the distant ruins of Cowdray.

Before setting off on the walk you may care to call at the Tourist Information Office to collect leaflets and maps of the town and surrounding area. There is a Midhurst Historic Town Trail which takes in 17 historic properties around the town in the

Cowdray now stands in ruins but when it was built in Tudor times it was one of the grandest houses in Sussex.

The fall of Cowdray was apparently foretold in a prophecy already two centuries old when fire gutted the mansion.

The walk north from Cowdray to Easebourne is by way of this broad, surfaced lane. The lane was installed to provide vehicular access to the polo grounds, but is abandoned to pedestrians when polo is not being played.

course of a walk that takes about half an hour to complete, plus time taken to visit the buildings in question - the two coaching inns are particularly tempting at lunchtime. It makes a useful and interesting addition to this more rural walk.

Cowdray had its origins in the 13th century when the old castle on St Ann's Hill was abandoned by the de Bohun family who owned extensive estates around here. The old castle was obsolete as a fortress and uncomfortable as a home, so a new fortified manor house was built at Coudreye on the far side of the river. In the early 16th century this was in turn pulled down by the Earl of Southampton who built the magnificent Tudor mansion, the ruins of which remain. Southampton sold the house to Sir Anthony Browne, Master of the Horse to King Henry VIII and his descendants, the Viscounts Montague.

The Montagues did not have an easy time of it. They were staunch Catholics at a time when the Pope wanted the Queen of England assassinated. In 1605 the famous Gunpowder Plot took place and although the Montagues had no direct role in that murderous scheme to kill King James I and all his ministers the fact that their servant Guy Fawkes was the man appointed to set the match to the gunpowder put them under grave suspicion. Viscount Montague spent 40 weeks in the Tower of London and had to pay a heavy fine to be released.

Despite their religion, the Montagues had gained their wealth largely through acquiring monastic lands when King Henry VIII dissolved the monasteries. The Abbot of Battle Abbey famously cursed Sir Anthony Browne declaring

The grandest house in Easebourne is that which was converted from the medieval Abbot's House. The parish church, formerly the monastic chapel, stands to the right.

that "By fire and water thy line shall come to an end and it shall perish out of the land." The curse is generally held to have come true in 1793 when the 8th Viscount drowned in the Rhine, his two sons drowned in a boating accident in Sussex and Cowdray itself was gutted by fire.

The ruins are now owned by the Cowdray Trust and are open to the public. There is an information centre and shop available.

2) After viewing the ruins of Cowdray, head north along the surfaced track that runs in front of the ruins.

3) At a fork in the track bear right. Follow this track north past the famous Cowdray Polo Field to emerge through a gate into a small car park with a large house and the parish church of Easebourne on your left. There is a rear door to the church here that is sometimes open. If it is enter the church, but if not continue on to the main road, then turn left to enter the churchyard through the lychgate and so enter the church through the north door.

This charming church is actually the chapel of Easebourne Priory, founded in 1248 by Sir Frank de Bohun who then owned Midhurst and surrounding lands. The Priory was to be home to 10 Benedictine nuns plus a Prioress and had lands endowed to it to provide for its upkeep. The church was built in two parts, one for the nuns and one for the parishioners of Easebourne. The tower and most of the church remain from this building.

Outside the church were built a guest house, cloisters, refectory and cells for the nuns. Most of these buildings remain standing to the south of the

The church at Easebourne stands in a large churchyard, formerly the grounds of the medieval Priory that once stood here.

The White Horse at Easebourne offers good lunches to the hungry traveller.

church, but are private houses and can be viewed only from the outside. In 1535 the Priory was closed down by King Henry VIII, its buildings and lands being bought by the owners of Cowdray. In August 1591 Queen Elizabeth I was passing and took lunch with Viscount Montague in the Refectory.

Through the centuries that followed little money was spent on the church and there was no vicar, only occasional services were held by a priest from Midhurst. In 1830 Stephen Poyntz, who had acquired Cowdray by marrying the daughter who inherited the estates, began some minor restoration work but it was in 1876 that the Earl of Egmont, who had bought the estate from Poyntz's daughter, began to spend serious money. The existing fabric was totally renovated, a new chancel added and the tower rebuilt. By 1925 the church stood much as it is today.

4) Leave the church by the north door and exit the churchyard via the lychgate. Turn left. The first turning on the right leads to the White Horse, a convivial pub serving good lunches. Continue along the pavement as the road bends left.

5) Walk along the pavement beside the road back to Midhurst. Cross the river and pass the Tourist Information Office and car park. Continue up the high street for about 150 yards to find Ye Olde Tea Shoppe on your left.

This is as fine a tea shop as you could hope to find. The tea itself is a joy. Not only is there straightforward Indian tea, but a range of Chinese and other teas is tempting, not to mention the various herbal brews on offer. The choice of coffees is just as wide. For those who are

Ye Olde Tea Shoppe in Midhurst is in a shop that was formerly home to the writer H.G. Wells.

The interior of Midhurst's Ye Olde Tea Shoppe is full of old world charm, as its name might suggest.

hungrier there is the traditional cream tea, a teacake tea, a crumpet tea or a croissant tea as set delights, plus a whole range of magnificent home-made cakes and pastries from which to choose. Ye Olde Tea Shoppe also offers a variety of sandwiches and baguettes as well as jacket potatoes and hot snacks, including no less than four types of Welsh Rarebit.

Coffee and walnut cake is just one of the many home-made treats on offer at Ye Olde Tea Shoppe.

The attractions of Ye Olde Tea Shoppe are not limited to its culinary delights. For many years this was the home of the novelist and science fiction writer H. G. Wells while he worked as a teacher at Midhurst Grammar School just down the road. The tea shop, which was then a sweetshop, features in several of his works including The Invisible Man, Tono-Bungay and The Man Who Could Work Miracles. Ye Olde Tea Shoppe offers Bed and Breakfast accommodation upstairs so readers especially keen on the works of H.G. Wells can stay in his old rooms for modest cost.

6) Having eaten your fill leave Ye Olde Tea Shoppe. Turn right to return to the car park where the walk began.

Midhurst's Grammar School is one of the most distinctive buildings on the High Street.

Walk No. 6 — Fishbourne

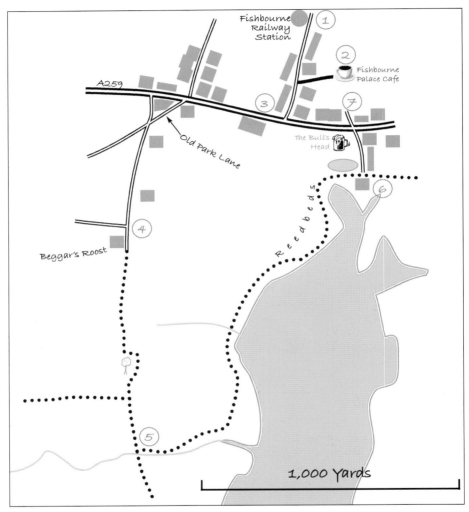

Fishbourne Railway Station

(1)

(2) Fishbourne Palace Cafe

A259

(3)

Old Park Lane

(7)

The Bull's Head

Reedbeds

(6)

(4)

Beggar's Roost

(5)

1,000 Yards

Ducks swim gently on the pond at Fishbourne.

6 Fishbourne

Distance:	**2.5 miles**
Route:	**Fishbourne**
Map:	**OS Explorer 120**
Teashop:	**Fishbourne Roman Palace Teashop**
Open:	**Daily 9.30 - 4.30**
Parking:	**There is a car park at Fishbourne Roman Palace.**
Public Transport:	**Fishbourne has a railway station and is served by several bus routes from central Chichester.**
Conditions:	**This walk is mostly over unsurfaced footpaths along the banks of the Fishbourne arm of Chichester Harbour. These paths can be muddy even in fairly dry weather. Elsewhere the route goes over paved paths.**

This gentle stroll is over entirely flat ground, most of which was formerly marsh drained in the 19th century. It starts and ends at Fishbourne railway station but moves on to the Roman Palace, possibly the most sumptuous villa in Roman Britain. There is little to see above ground now, but the stunning mosaics have survived almost intact and are now preserved under cover. The adjacent museum preserves many finds made during the excavation of the site.

The Walk

1) Find your way to Fishbourne railway station. Leave the platform by way of the level crossing and turn right to walk south along the lane. Turn left into Roman Way, signposted to the Roman Palace. At the end of this residential lane is a car park, Fishbourne Palace and the Palace Tea Rooms.

The walk starts and finishes at Fishbourne's small railway station.

In 1960 a workman digging a trench unearthed some small coloured stones. These were recognised as being Roman mosaic tessarae and the archaeologists were called in. What they found was simply astonishing. Buried beneath the Sussex fields was the largest Roman palace in Britain, possibly the largest single building north of the Alps at the time it was completed in around

The tea rooms at Fishbourne are housed in the rather functional building that protects the ruins of the mighty Roman palace found here in the 1960s.

The turning to the Roman Palace is clearly signposted from the main road.

South of Beggar's Roost the walk follows a path across open farmland that was marshland until fairly recently.

AD75. It covered six acres, with more probably being given over to ancillary buildings such as stables and storehouses.

Not only was the palace big, it was luxurious in the extreme and completed to the very highest standards. The floors of the living quarters were decorated with mosaics as good as any in the Roman Empire, the boy riding a dolphin is perhaps the best in Britain. The palace was clearly home to somebody both rich and powerful, but there were no clues in the ruins as to who that might have been.

Historians went through their records and came up with the name of King Cogidubnus. The British monarch ruled the Regni tribe of Celts who occupied this section of the South Coast at the time. Cogidubnus had welcomed the Roman invasion in AD43 as it freed his tribe from the control of the Catuvellauni tribe of the Thames Valley. Clearly Roman overlordship of the Regni was less onerous than that of their fellow Celts. Once the invasion was over, Cogidubnus was invited to visit Rome where the Emperor Claudius made a great fuss of him, appointing him to be a Senator of Rome.

It seems likely that on his return Cogidubnus had the Fishbourne Palace built for him by way of a thank you for his help. The palace included a monumental staircase to a large room under an impressive portico. Most likely this was the chamber where King Cogidubnus carried out his royal duties.

The palace remained a residence of luxury and taste until AD280 when a fire broke out. Thereafter, the remaining rooms were taken over by farmers and craftsmen, the rich owners presumably preferring to move to a new home elsewhere, perhaps in the nearby city of Noviomagus, now Chichester.

Today the North Wing of the palace is open to visitors. It is protected by a large building to shelter the mosaics and walls from the elements. The East and West Wings have been excavated, but were re-covered to protect the fragile remains. The South Wing lies under the houses of Fishbourne village and

Long lines of trees act as windbreaks on the flat, open fields that border the sea south of Fishbourne.

so has not been excavated.

The adjacent teashop is housed in a building best described as functional. It offers a variety of snacks and biscuits suited to the tastes and pockets of the large numbers of children who come here on school trips, but also keeps a range of finer and more delicious tea fare. There are always at least three tasty home-made cakes on the counter and other pastries and cakes can be rustled up from the kitchens.

2) Having visited the Roman palace and tea shop return along Roman Way. At the lane turn left to head south away from the railway station.

3) At the main road, the A259, turn right and walk along the pavement beside the road for about 400 yards. Bear left into Old Park Road. At a crossroads ignore the route straight on, which is little more than a surfaced track, and instead bear left. Follow this lane south over flat, open fields. This land was all marsh in Roman times.

4) Where the lane turns suddenly right in front of the large house named Beggar's Roost, continue straight on along a gravel track. This track soon deteriorates into an earth footpath

A fallen poplar causes the path to deviate from its previous route close to a ditch on the drained farmland.

A distant view of Chichester Cathedral can be had from the walk as it crosses farmland south of Fishbourne.

A charming thatched cottage in Fishbourne.

The Bull's Head in Fishbourne offers good lunches to hungry walkers.

As the walk returns north toward Fishbourne it follows the top of the earth bank that protects the farmland from flooding at high tides.

As the walk picks its way through the extensive reedbeds it crosses over several small streams by way of wooden footbridges such as this.

When the walk reaches this extensive freshwater pond it turns left off the footpath and on to a narrow lane.

running beside a hedge across open fields. Continue south as the path jinks left then right to avoid a small copse in which lurks a pond. Ignore the path turning off to the right.

5) Turn left along a footpath beside a ditch and follow this path until it reaches an earthen sea wall. Climb up the bank and continue along the path as it bends to the north. The path runs along the top of the sea wall for some distance. It then comes down off the sea wall by way of some wooden steps and strikes out across damp reedbeds. The path here is surfaced and wooden bridges cross the numerous streams but it can still be slippery in wet weather.

6) The path eventually leaves the reed beds, passing a large open pond on the left and a house on the right. It then meets a narrow lane lined by houses. Turn left up this lane to reach the Bull's Head, a welcoming tavern that serves hot and tasty lunches.

At the time the Fishbourne Palace was built this area stood at the very head of Chichester Harbour. A busy wharf was built here by the Roman army at which supplies for the invading troops could be landed. Once the war was over, the wharf was taken over for civilian use and formed the basis of the prosperity of Noviomagus, which grew rapidly from a small army depot to be a large fortified city. The A259 follows roughly the route of the Roman road from docks to city.

7) Turn left at the A259, then right to return to the railway station where the walk began.

Walk No. 7

Battle

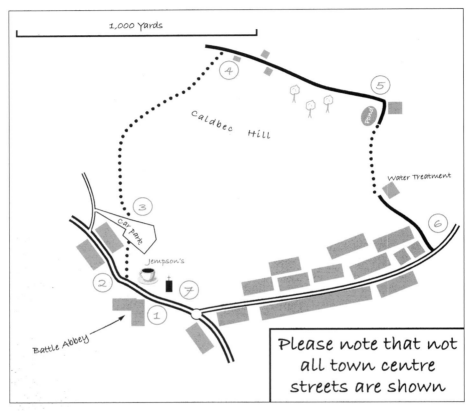

1,000 Yards

Caldbec Hill

Water Treatment

Pond

car park

Jempson's

Battle Abbey

Please note that not all town centre streets are shown

The massive gatehouse to Battle Abbey dominates the town and makes a convenient spot from which to start the walk.

7 Battle

Distance:	**3 miles**
Route:	**Battle - Caldbec Hill - Battle**
Map:	**OS Explorer 124**
Teashop:	**Jempson's Cafe, 78 High Street, Battle.**
Parking:	**There are two car parks and limited on-street parking in Battle.**
Public Transport:	**Battle is on the mainline railway.**
Conditions:	**This walk is partly over unsurfaced paths across pastureland that can be muddy after rain, and partly along roadside pavements in the town centre.**

Battle is, of course, best known for the Battle of Hastings which was fought here in 1066. The forces of Duke William of Normandy defeated the English under King Harold II, killing that warrior king in the late afternoon of that fateful 14 October. What is not generally known is that the victorious Normans were ambushed as dusk fell and suffered a defeat just north of the battlefield, though this setback was not enough to stop William seizing the English throne and with it the sobriquet of "the Conqueror". This walk takes in the sites of both the main battle and the later ambush.

The Walk

1) In Battle find the massive gatehouse of Battle Abbey which dominates the town centre and is signposted from both car parks and from the railway station.

This gatehouse has some walls dating to the 12th century, but was almost entirely rebuilt in around 1340 and most of what can be seen today dates from that time. The upper floor is filled by a grand hall, while the ground floor has smaller, functional rooms such as the porter's lodge and storerooms. The Abbey grounds are open to the public, though a charge is made. If you wish to explore the Abbey and its grounds enter through the main gate at the centre of the gatehouse.

The Abbey was founded by King William the Conqueror to mark the spot where he had defeated and killed King Harold II in the famous Battle of Hastings, fought on 14th October

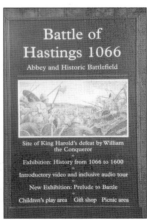

The town of Battle is named for the Battle of Hastings that took place here in 1066, as commemorated on this information board outside the Abbey.

1066. William died before the abbey was completed, so it was his son William II who presided over the dedication of the church to St Martin in 1094. Of this original, rather modest, monastery nothing now stands above ground as it was completely rebuilt on a much grander scale during the 13th century.

In 1538 the monastery at Battle shared the fate of all the English monasteries and was closed down by King Henry VIII as part of his reformation of the Church of England, then newly separated from the authority of the Pope in Rome. The monastery was handed over to Sir Anthony Browne, Master of the King's Horse who also owned Cowdray (see Walk 5 Midhurst). Browne promptly had the church pulled down and sold off the stone, glass and other materials for cash. He kept the Abbot's lodging, gatehouse and other buildings for his own home, converting and adapting them for family use as necessary.

Turning off the High Street the walk goes down this narrow lane towards a car park.

Over the centuries that followed the buildings were altered, rebuilt and renovated many times to suit changing fashions and the changing fortunes of the property's owners. Of the medieval abbey much is still to be seen. Fragments of the cloisters still stand, while the parlour, dorter and dining chambers still stand. The main survivor is the Abbot's House, which became the main residence of Sir Anthony Browne. A severe fire caused much damage in 1933, but this has since been repaired.

The walk exits the car park by way of this footpath that runs between the gardens of two houses.

William the Conqueror insisted that the high altar of the church should be built on the precise spot where the body of King Harold was found, surrounded by those of his loyal warriors, after the battle. The site is now marked by an impressive monument, the Harold Stone, erected in 1903.

The grounds of the Abbey include most of the hill held by the English army and the slope up which the Normans attacked, though the flanks of the English position lie outside the grounds as does the position taken up by William and his men when the battle began. Information boards and markings help the visitor to find their way around the battlefield.

2) Having explored the Abbey leave the gatehouse and walk straight on northwest along the High Street of the town of Battle. There are several pubs in the High Street serving lunches and dinners. About 200 yards along the High Street from the gatehouse an alley with an iron arch over it turns off to the right.

The view north from Caldbec Hill. It was somewhere near here that a group of Norman knights came to grief in the aftermath of the battle.

This is Abbey Court. Follow the alley as it passes some shops, then bends left in front of houses to emerge into a car park.

3) Cross the car park to find a footpath that leaves the car park beside a wooden fence and a house named Little Twitten. Follow this path between some houses then across a lane to run beside some lock-up garages and so to emerge into open fields. The path then goes up Caldbec Hill and emerges on to a surfaced track just over the crest of the hill.

4) Turn right along this lane which has a few houses scattered along it but is mostly bordered by open fields and small patches of woodland.

The lane along the summit of Caldbec Hill ends soon after it crosses this rather overgrown bridge across a railway.

It was somewhere along here that disaster struck a group of victorious Norman knights on the evening of the battle. King Harold had been killed shortly before sunset and although his personal bodyguard of professional warriors chose to fight on to the death, the bulk of the English army began to break up and retreat northward. After the remaining English warriors were killed, the mounted Norman knights began the pursuit of the fleeing English army.

As the Normans came over the crest of Caldbec Hill one group stumbled into a narrow gully or defile. The cohesion of the knights was broken and a few fell from their horses. A group of retreating English saw their chance and attacked. Several Norman knights were killed in the confused fighting that followed. William called off the pursuit until the next day, allowing many more English to escape than might otherwise have been the case.

Returning to Battle from Caldbec Hill the walk passes down this footpath hemmed in by wire fencing.

But William was undoubtedly the winner. Harold's young sons fled into exile and William was crowned King of England on Christmas Day. The battle fought at Battle was the decisive event of the Norman invasion.

5) Continue along the lane that runs along the summit of Caldbec Hill. It narrows to cross a railway bridge, then turns sharp right to pass between a pond and farm buildings. The lane then ends, but continues as a footpath that runs south between two wire fences. Follow this path downhill to emerge onto another surfaced lane beside a water treatment works. Follow the lane to reach a road at a T-junction.

6) Turn right along this road, passing under a railway bridge to reach a mini-roundabout. Continue straight on and climb up to return to the town centre. Immediately before reaching the Abbey gatehouse Jempson's Cafe will be found on the right.

Jempson's is unusual among tea shops in that it is self-service. Trays can be collected to the left of the door as you enter and there is a stunningly tempting array of cakes, pastries

At a water treatment works the walk picks up this surfaced track that carries it over a small hill and down to a lane.

Jempson's is to be found in Battle High Street, just east of the Abbey Gatehouse.

and light meals all made on the premises from which to choose. Tea, coffee and other drinks are served from a counter beside the cash till opposite the front door. Behind the till is a comfortable lounge and beyond that a fine courtyard equipped with tables and chairs for use in fine weather.

7) After taking tea, leave Jempson's and bear right to return to the Abbey gatehouse where the walk began.

Jempson's serves a truly delicious cream tea.

Walk No. 8   Alfriston

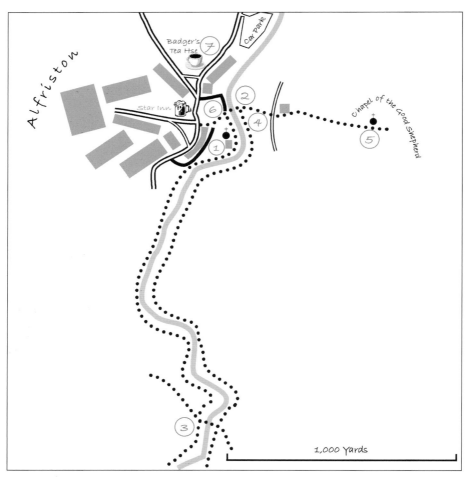

Alfriston's medieval Clergy House was the first house ever to be owned by the National Trust. The Trust own it still and it is open to the public.

8 Alfriston

Distance:	**3.75 miles**
Route:	**Alfriston - Chapel of the Good Shepherd - Alfriston**
Map:	**OS Explorer 123**
Teashop:	**Badger's Tea House, 12 North Street, Alfriston**
Open:	**Daily 9 - 4.30**
Parking:	**There is a car park and very limited on-street parking in Alfriston.**
Public Transport:	**Alfriston is served by the Renown Coaches Bus route 126 from Eastbourne.**
Conditions:	**This walk is mostly over unsurfaced paths, though the sections in the village are on roadside pavements. The section alongside the Cuckmere River can be damp or muddy at almost any time.**

The little town of Alfriston is one of the quaintest in Sussex and during the summer months is a target for day trips run by coach companies from the nearby seaside resorts of Brighton, Eastbourne and Bexhill. Most of the daytrippers remain in the town centre with its historic properties and few penetrate over the river to enjoy the beautiful scenery through which this walk wanders.

The Walk

1) In Alfriston find the parish church, which lies off the southern end of the high street next to the National Trust property, the Clergy House, which is well signposted.

The church dominates the green which it overlooks and by its sheer size overshadows all other churches in the area. Indeed, it has become known locally as the Cathedral of the Downs due to its size and majesty. Unlike most other old English churches, Alfriston's Church of St Andrew was built all in one

Alfriston church stands on a slight rise above the large village green.

The walk leaves the green around the church through these posts and bears right down toward the river.

The walk heads south alongside the Cuckmere River following the signposts for this gentle and well-marked route.

The Cuckmere River south of Alfriston is a gentle stream that meanders lazily through water meadows.

go, in the 1360s, and has not seen any major alterations since. It is known that there was a timber church here in around 780 and a stone one was put up in the Norman period, but no trace of these remain. They may not even have stood on the site of the modern church for the old cemetery lay in what is now Winton Street.

According to local legend, the villagers wanted to put their church to the west of the main village street. The flints were knapped and piled up ready for construction work to begin, but when the workmen arrived on the appointed day the stones had all been moved by some supernatural force to the small hill above the green. Beside the stones were four oxen sitting with their rumps touching so as to form a cross. Taking this to be divine intervention, the builders put the church where it now stands.

Those medieval craftsmen built with great care. Most flint structures have only the exterior face of the flints knapped to be flat. The interior of the walls are a jumble of misshapen flint nodules all held together by large amounts of mortar. Not so at St Andrew's Church. The stones are all knapped to be square and any gaps filled with flint chips rather than mortar. No other large building was completed in this labour-intensive fashion. The construction stood firm for five centuries until Victorian times when the modern pointing was inserted to bind together loose stones.

Although the main fabric of the church has not altered much, the interior has. Box pews were put in, then taken out again. A gallery inserted, removed and then replaced. A reredos was likewise installed, altered and finally removed.

The stained glass is magnificent and dates mostly to 1877 or 1904 and CE Kemp and James Powell were at work here respectively.

The Clergy House next door to the church was built in the 1380s. It may have been intended as a home for the clergy, but more likely was rented out to provide income for the church. In 1895 it was bought for £10 by the National Trust. The purchase was something of a landmark as the Trust had previously owned only land and coastline. The acquisition of a house was a new direction for the Trust.

The tiny Chapel of the Good Shepherd is the smallest parish church in Sussex.

2) Leave the green in front of the church at its northern end by way of a path between two posts. Follow the path down to the Cuckmere River to find the White Bridge, a footbridge over the river that is painted white. Just before the bridge turn right along a footpath that

is signposted as "The Kissing Gate Walk", so named as there are no stiles only kissing gates along its route. Follow the well-signed walk along the banks of the Cuckmere for well over a mile.

3) At a footbridge, cross the Cuckmere towards the village of Litlington. Immediately beyond the bridge turn left to return along the east bank of the Cuckmere along the return branch of the Kissing Gate Walk.

4) At the White Bridge, turn right across the water meadows. Cross a road, jinking right to continue along the footpath beside a house. This path strikes over open fields uphill to a small wood in which is hidden the tiny Chapel of the Good Shepherd.

This is the parish church for the village of Lullington, though it has been joined to Alfriston for almost a century now. The church is widely recognised as the smallest parish church in Sussex, being only 16 feet square. In fact this is the chancel of what was once

The walk returns over the Cuckmere to Alfriston by way of the aptly named White Bridge.

a much larger church, a few broken stones of which can be seen in the churchyard west of the standing church. The 13th century church was burnt down courtesy of passing Roundhead troopers during the civil war of the 1640s. Famously Puritan in their faith these troopers took exception to some images in the church that they considered idolatrous.

5) Leave the church and return to the White Bridge. Cross the bridge and turn immediately right along a surfaced track. This then bends left away from the river to pass between houses to reach the market square. Turn right down North Street. The Badger's Tea House

A scrumptious Victoria Sandwich (left) and a magnificent Blueberry Layer Cake (above), just two of the many home-made cakes regularly baked at the Badger's Tea Rooms.

Badger's Tea House is located in a house just north of the Market Square.

is to be found on the left after about 75 yards.

The range of cakes to be found here is truly astonishing. The owner prides himself on his innovative approach to cake making and has produced some truly wonderful confections using fresh fruit, cream and a range of other delicious ingredients. Like the cakes, the biscuits, scones and pastries are also home-made on the premises and taste truly delicious. The staff are friendly and helpful, making a stop here a most enjoyable experience.

7) After sampling the tasty treats on offer, leave the Badger's Tea House. Turn left to head south along North Street. Cross the Market Square and continue along the High Street. Both the St George's Tavern on the left and the Star Inn on the right are welcoming hostelries that serve tasty lunches. Continue south, then turn left to return to the church where the walk began.

Alfriston's Market Square stands at the northern end of the High Street.

The Star Inn offers delicious lunches and suppers.

Walk No. 9   Ditchling

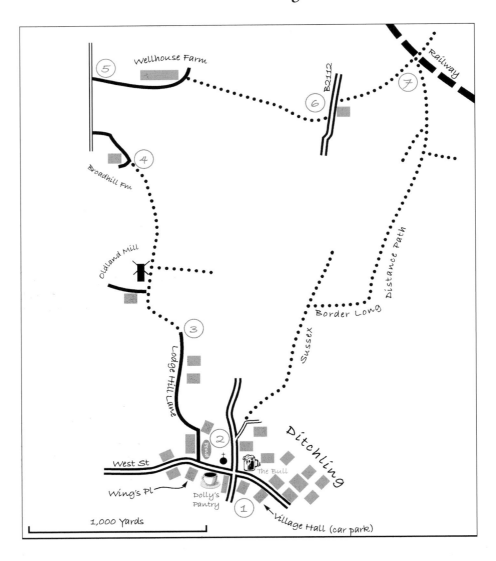

9 Ditchling

Distance:	**4.3 miles**
Route:	**Ditchling - Broadhill - Ditchling**
Map:	**OS Explorer 122**
Teashop:	**Dolly's Pantry, 6 West St, Ditchling.**
Open:	**Monday - Saturday 10 - 4.30**
Parking:	**There is a car park in Ditchling and limited on-street parking.**
Public Transport:	**Ditchling is served by the Countryliner Coach route 824 from Lewes.**
Conditions:	**This walk is mostly over unsurfaced paths, though these are generally fairly good. There are no steep hills to be encountered.**

Ditchling is a charming village of some size nestling at the foot of the South Downs where those hills plunge down into the Weald. Part of this walk follows the Sussex Border Path across open fields. There is one gentle hill to be negotiated, but it is only slight and should present no difficulties.

The Walk

1) The main car park stands behind the Village Hall and is well signposted. Exit the car park and turn left to walk past The Bull public house on your right. The Bull is a welcoming place serving good lunches and teas. At the crossroads go straight ahead into West Street. Dolly's Pantry is on your left.

This charming teashop comes in two parts. There is the shop through which you enter where you can buy truly delicious cakes, pastries and other delights. The tea rooms are to the right and offer a comfortable range of seats and tables. There is a patio at the rear which is used in good weather. The range of teatime treats on offer is impressive, and the Sussex Cream Tea comes with scones that are both large and delicious. On selected days Dolly's is open into the evening when tasty

The magnificent cream tea served at Dolly's Pantry.

Wing's Place was built for Henry VIII's queen Catherine of Aragon as part of her divorce settlement, but she did not care for it and never lived here.

Ditchling's parish church goes back certainly over a thousand years and may stand on the site of a pagan religious centre as many as 3,000 years old.

suppers are served up to those who can secure a table.

2) Leaving Dolly's turn left along West Street. On your left you will see Wing's Place while on the right is St Margaret's Church.

Wing's Place is a magnificent Tudor manor house. It is a private residence and not open to the public, but it can be studied from the outside. This house was built on the orders of King Henry VIII for his queen, Catherine of Aragon. This was no love gift, however, as Henry was in the process of annulling his marriage to Catherine at the time. Henry had tired of Catherine who was getting past childbearing age and had not given him a son. Henry wanted to marry the pretty young Anne Boleyn who he hoped would give him a male heir. Catherine was, however, the daughter of the King of Spain and had to be treated tactfully if there were not to be an open break.

Henry therefore endowed Catherine with numerous manors and estates to provide her with an income. It was as part of this campaign that Wing's Place was built.

Unfortunately Catherine did not care for the place. She turned the house over to be an office from which managers could run her estates in Sussex. She herself went to live at Ampthill in Bedfordshire. There she lived in comfort, but kept up her opposition to Anne Boleyn and refused to accept that the annulment of their marriage was legal. She died in 1536 and is buried at Peterborough Cathedral.

The pond in Ditchling lies below the church and beside a prehistoric trackway along which the walk leaves the village.

The Church of St Margaret is considerably older than Wing's Place. The West Wall contains flint work that is about 1100 years old and much of the standing structure is from the 11th century, though the chancel was built two centuries later. In fact the site might be the oldest sacred place in Sussex. The churchyard wall contains some enigmatic boulders that some archaeologists believe to be the remnants of a prehistoric henge or temple composed of upright stones set in a circle. If so, then the local people have been worshipping on this little knoll for over 3,000 years.

Certainly the hill was used as a burial place by the pagan Saxons who settled here after the fall of the Roman Empire. Their leader, Dicul, gave his name to the village in about 491. It is generally thought that the skeleton of a tall Saxon unearthed here during Victorian renovation works was that of Dicul.

3) Just west of the church lies a pond. Heading north off West Street immediately west of the pond is a surfaced track known as Lodge Hill Lane. Follow this lane as it wanders generally northward past several houses interspersed with farmland. The track eventually peters out to become a footpath tending more northwest. The path meets a lane at Oldland Windmill. Ignore the lane and continue along the path heading north.

This track is one of the oldest in Sussex. Archaeologists have found flint arrowheads and other Neolithic remains beside the track. It is thought that this was a trade route by which flints from the chalk downlands were carried north to areas that did not have natural sources of this most useful of stones. The flints would be exchanged for food,

At the top of Lodge Hill, the lane peters out and gradually becomes a footpath heading north.

After passing Oldland Mill the walk descends a hill to Broadhill Farm passing through a copse of trees immediately before reaching a surfaced lane.

furs and other goods that were brought back south along the track.

4) At Broadhill Farm the path joins a track that then meets a lane at a T-junction. Turn left up the lane.

5) After a hundred yards or so turn right up Wellhouse Lane towards Wellhouse Farm. The lane ends after the farm buildings, but a signed footpath continues over farmland and up a gentle slope. This path eventually emerges on to the B2112.

6) The B2112 is surprisingly busy for a B road so care should be taken in crossing it. Once over the road bear left to find a stile to the left of a large house. Climb over this stile and follow a footpath heading over the pasture fields to the northeast.

7) This path eventually comes to the London-Seaford railway line which it crosses by way of a footbridge. Immediately before the footbridge turn right along the well-signed Sussex Border Path, a long distance footpath cared for by the County Council. Follow the Sussex Border Path back to Ditchling Village, emerging into the High Street a few yards north of The Bull. Turn left, then left again to return to the car park where the walk began.

After crossing the B2112 the walk goes over this stile to enter a field and run northeast toward a railway cutting.

As it nears Ditchling the Sussex Border Path weaves between first allotments and then gardens before emerging in the village centre.

Walk No. 10   *Stanmer*

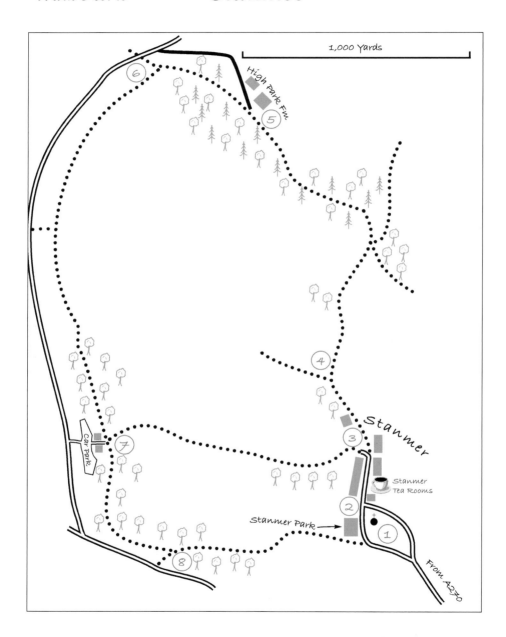

10 Stanmer

Distance:	**4.3 miles**
Route:	**Stanmer - High Park - Stanmer**
Map:	**OS Explorer 122**
Teashop:	**Stanmer Tea Rooms, Stanmer Park, Stanmer.**
Open:	**Daily 9.30 - 4.30**
Parking:	**There is a car park just outside Stanmer where the walk begins and ends.**
Public Transport:	**Stanmer is served by the Brighton & Hove Bus and Coach Company Bus 25 from central Brighton.**
Conditions:	**This walk is mostly over unsurfaced paths through woodland on the South Downs. The surfaces are generally good, but broken in places. There is one fairly high but not excessively steep hill to be climbed.**

Stanmer Park, an old manor and its tied village just to the north of Brighton, was in private hands until 1947 when it was bought in its entirety by Brighton Council. The house itself is now a conference venue and the cottages are private houses, but the surrounding woodlands were opened to the public and part of this walk runs through them before striking off to run over farmland and other woodland to reach High Park Farm before returning to Stanmer by way of open downland.

The Walk

1) Once in Stanmer Park make your way to the extensive green that stretches between the main house and the church.

The house was built in 1722 as home to the local Pelham family. The most famous member of the family was their second son, the prominent statesman the Hon. Henry Pelham, Prime Minister of Great Britain from 1743 to 1754. Henry Pelham had first attracted attention by his bravery and efficiency when fighting against the Jacobite

The house at Stanmer Park was built for one of Sussex's premier families, but they sold up in 1947 and moved to Wiltshire.

The gate that gives access to the churchyard at Stanmer is overgrown and never closed.

Rebellion of 1715 which aimed to restore the Stuart dynasty to the thrones of England, Scotland and Ireland. His martial skills saw him rise to be Minister for War in 1724. Thereafter he held a variety of posts before becoming Prime Minister. As premier

The grave of the 8th Earl of Chichester, killed during the Second World War, lies in Stanmer churchyard.

he oversaw the defeat of the 1745 Jacobite Uprising led by Bonnie Prince Charlie and took Britain into the War of the Austrian Succession.

It was a descendant, Thomas Pelham, also a politician being MP for Rye, who in 1801 was honoured when he was created Earl of Chichester in the Peerage of the United Kingdom. The family has been distinguished in English history, supplying a number of bishops, government officials and others over the years. The 8th Earl was killed on active service in 1944 and lies buried in the churchyard. His only child was a son born two months later who thus became the 9th Earl of Chichester the moment he was born.

The house was for a time the administrative centre for the University of Sussex, but that institution now has purpose-built accommodation and a spreading campus half a mile to the east, built over much of the Stanmer Park estates. The main house is open to the public on Tuesday mornings, and at other times is available for hire for weddings, conferences and the like.

The estate of Stanmer Park included not just the house and its park land but also the village of Stanmer with its church and cottages as well as extensive farmland. The church was entirely rebuilt in 1838, the older 14th century structure being deemed to be beyond repair. It is usually locked.

Stanmer Church was built in the early 19th century to replace an earlier structure that had fallen into disrepair.

2) From the green head north along a lane with the church on your right. Just past a turning to the right the Stanmer Park Tea Rooms stand on the right of the road.

The tea rooms are spacious and comfortable. There is an open court in front for use in the summer months, and two large rooms inside for less clement weather. The home-made cakes are delicious, as are the scones, and the tea is served piping hot.

3) Leaving the tea rooms, turn right to walk through Stanmer Village itself. At the end of the lane there is a choice. To follow the longer walk you will need to pass through a gate and head straight on to the north along a track past a barn on the left. To follow the shorter version, follow the lane as it bends left. Then go through a second gate and follow a surfaced track past a wood. This track eventually comes out at point 7 in the longer walk.

4) Following the track past the barn you will come to a Y junction. Take the right hand fork and follow this for some distance up a gentle slope to enter a wood. At the edge of the woodland is an irregular crossroads of tracks. Turn left and walk through the woods toward High Park Farm.

5) At High Park Farm ignore the surfaced drive that leads away from the farm buildings and instead bear left along a footpath through the trees in a line roughly parallel to the farm driveway.

6) Just before you reach a lane, turn left down a footpath signposted to New Barn. Follow this clear footpath through some woods then out on to open downland. Pass a park bench

The Stanmer Tea Rooms have a small patio where tea may be taken in good weather.

Scones are a speciality of the Stanmer Tea Rooms.

thoughtfully provided for walkers. Continue along the path as it re-enters woodland, now heading due south.

7) In the woodland the footpath crosses a surfaced track. To the right are a pair of houses, the original gatehouses to Stanmer Park Estate, and a car park. To the left the track runs back to point 3 on the walk. This is where the shorter version of the walk emerges. Continue straight on south, staying on the footpath as it bends left to run alongside a lane.

These woods are famously full of bats. During the summer guided walks are on offer at dusk so that visitors can see the bats in flight and inspect their roosts.

8) The footpath skirts a second car park then becomes a surfaced track as it runs from the car park back to Stanmer Park. Walk past the main house to return to the green where the walk began.

One of the scenic cottages to be found in Stanmer.

The shorter of the two routes on this walk leaves Stanmer Village by way of this gate.

The longer walk at Stanmer climbs up on to the open downs where the Council has thoughtfully provided some benches on which a rest may be taken.

Walk No. 11 Winchelsea

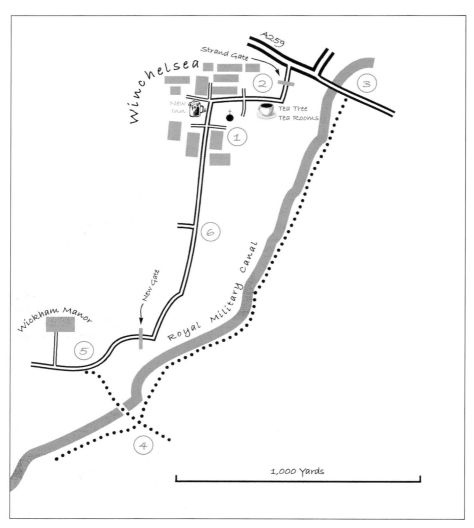

A259

Strand Gate

Winchelsea

② ③

New Inn

Tea Tree Tea Rooms

①

⑥

New Gate

Wickham Manor

Royal Military Canal

⑤

④

1,000 Yards

JOHN WESLEY
Preached his last Open Air Sermon
here, on 7th October 1790
Wesley's Chapel 1st left, then left again

A sign screwed to a tree by the churchyard reminds the passer-by that this small village was once rather more important that it is today.

11 *Winchelsea*

Distance:	**3.5 miles**
Route:	**Winchelsea - Wickham - Winchelsea**
Map:	**OS Explorer 125**
Teashop:	**Tea Tree Tea Rooms, 12 High Street, Winchelsea**
Parking:	**There is on-street parking in Winchelsea.**
Public Transport:	**Winchelsea is served by the railway, though the station is a mile or so from the town centre where the walk begins.**
Conditions:	**This walk is partly along quiet lanes and partly along a section of the Saxon Shore Way long distance footpath which, while unsurfaced, is well maintained. There are no steep hills or difficult terrain.**

Winchelsea was one of the most important ports in Sussex during the 13th century until a savage raid by the French and silt in the harbour combined to render it useless. The town is now no larger than many villages, but it retains part of its huge church and some of its fortifications. This walk takes in the key sights of Winchelsea as well as a stretch of the Royal Military Canal that passes close by.

The Walk

1) Once in Winchelsea find the church that stands in the centre of a huge churchyard off the High Street.

The most obvious feature about St Thomas' Church is that it is surrounded by ruins. In fact the church that stands today is merely the chancel and adjacent chapel of the much larger original, destroyed by the French during a 14th century raid. The good folk of Winchelsea always intended to rebuild their lost church, but they never got round to it as the town

The charming church at Winchelsea is but a fraction of a much larger edifice that stood here in medieval times.

The Winchelsea Museum is located in Court Hall opposite the church. This is the oldest structure still standing in Winchelsea having been begun in 1288.

Winchelsea's Tea Tree Tea Rooms stand in the High Street north of the churchyard.

The start of the path along the Royal Military Canal is indicated by this signpost beside the road to Winchelsea Beach.

was set on a downward spiral of declining prosperity.

Ironically the problem was not the French, but the sea. The town of Winchelsea originally stood about a mile or so east of the current site at what was then the mouth of the River Brede. It was a thriving port and secure harbour that handled much of the export trade for Sussex. Like Rye (see Walk 16) it was part of the Cinque Ports organisation. Then, in 1287, a devastating storm swept the area. The sea wall was breached by waves coming in from the sea while the town was engulfed by flood waters coming down the Brede. When the weather calmed down the inhabitants crept out to find that their world had changed. The secure harbour had gone entirely, several houses had vanished into the sea and what was left of the town was clearly doomed to go the same way.

King Edward I came down to survey the damage and decided that a new town had to be built. He chose the top of Hiham Hill and ordered the construction of a new town wall pierced by four powerful gatehouses as well as a new harbour at the foot of the hill. The grateful inhabitants of Winchelsea hurried to build new houses, warehouses and docking facilities on the new site. Within five years Winchelsea was fully open for business once again. Prosperity and wealth poured in.

But as the sea created the new town, so it was to undermine it. By about 1450 the sea was retreating once again. It no longer lapped the foot of Hiham Hill but was retreating away to the south and east leaving mud flats and salt marsh in its place. The harbour at what had been the mouth of the Brede in 1390 was now some distance upstream from the new mouth of the river. For some years the Winchelsea authorities had the river regularly dredged out so that ships could reach the harbour but by the mid-16th century the task had become too great. They gave up the effort and the port closed to seagoing ships. The population nosedived as merchants, shipbuilders, chandlers and the like moved elsewhere.

Strand Gate is one of the three original gateways into Winchelsea that remain standing.

The Royal Military Canal sweeps away from Winchelsea heading west.

An echo of the former greatness of Winchelsea as a port can be seen inside the church. The tomb of England's first admiral, Gervase Alard, lies in a small alcove.

2) Leaving the church turn right to walk across the extensive churchyard to reach the High Street. Turn right. About 40 yards beyond the end of the churchyard you will find the Tea Tree Tea Rooms and Gift Shop on your right.

This is a traditional tea room at its very finest. Set in an ancient building, the tea rooms offer beautiful home-made cakes and pastries served on good china with dainty napkins. The tea itself is served nice and fresh with little china milk jugs and sugar bowls to hand. There is also a range of lunch treats on offer and morning coffee is every bit as impressive as the afternoon tea.

3) Having taken tea, leave the Tea Tree Tea Rooms and turn right along High Street. At the end of High Street the road bends sharp left and then passes through the Strand Gate, one of those built by Edward I. The road drops steeply down Strand Hill to meet the A259 at the foot of the hill. Directly in front of you on the other side of the main road is a row of

A swan rests beside the Royal Military Canal. The waterway is a haven for wildlife and attracts many birdwatchers.

The walk turns right to cross the Royal Military Canal over this rather basic bridge.

The site of an artillery emplacement defending the Royal Military Canal. The view is that which would have been had by the gunners as they aimed their cannon along the canal.

The walk climbs up a slight slope after crossing the Royal Military Canal to reach a lane.

houses that occupies the site of the docks and warehouses built by Edward I. The River Brede lies just beyond them. Turn right along the A259, then after barely 50 yards go straight on as the main road bends left. This lane is signposted to Winchelsea Beach. The beach is about a mile distant and although not on this walk is worth a visit in the summer months. Within 50 yards of leaving the A259 the lane crosses the Royal Military Canal by way of a bridge. Turn right through a gate on the far side of the canal to join the towpath.

Unlike most canals this was never intended to have commercial barges plying up and down it. This was a defensive work designed to repel a French invasion of Britain. In 1804 the French Emperor Napoleon I was the master of Europe. He had defeated or allied himself to every state on the continent. Only one country stood between him and world domination: Britain. The British Empire spread over much of the world while British merchants and ships dominated world trade. And the powerful Royal Navy blocked French ambitions overseas. Only by invading Britain, Napoleon reasoned, could he break Britain's commercial and naval might. In 1804 he began gathering an invasion army around Calais and Boulogne.

The British Navy responded by blockading the French ports and preparing to take on the French navy should an invasion fleet put to sea. A chain of coastal forts known as Martello Towers was begun to guard harbours and isolated landing beaches (see Walk 17 Seaford), but the long, low-lying coastline of the Romney Marsh peninsula between Winchelsea and Hythe offered real problems. The wide open beaches meant that a French army could land almost anywhere. Rather than try to defend the long coastline, the British army decided to shorten the line to be defended by digging a fortified canal across the neck of the peninsula.

Work on the canal began in 1804 and took five years to complete. The canal was 28 miles long, ten feet deep and up to 60 feet wide. The earth dug out of the canal was piled up behind it to form an earthen wall with a parapet and firing step so that it could be manned by infantry armed with muskets. In front of the canal were dug various pits and water-filled trenches to make if difficult for the French to bring up artillery or cavalry with which to assault the canal. At intervals along the canal were constructed artillery positions from which British gunners could fire at attackers while themselves being protected by earthworks.

In the event the French never invaded. Led by Lord Nelson the Royal Navy crushed the French navy at the Battle of Trafalgar. Nevertheless the canal was to become a permanent feature of the landscape. Farmers found it to be a very useful drainage channel. Large areas of Romney Marsh were drained by ditches that emptied into the Royal Military Canal, and the salt marshes around Winchelsea were turned into productive pasture land.

In more recent years, the canal has become a favourite destination for those interested in wildlife. Swans, herons, moorhens and other wetland birds are to be found here in numbers, as can frogs, toads, newts, dragonflies and a host of other wildlife.

New Gate marked the southern end of Winchelsea as it was built after the old town fell into the sea after a 13th century storm.

4) Continue along the canalside path for about a mile until you find a footbridge crossing the canal and a path crossing both the canal and the path on which you are walking. Turn right to cross the bridge through a pair of gates. Once over the canal continue across a field and round a small clump of trees to reach a lane.

As you cross the canal you will be walking through one of the artillery bastions inserted at intervals to defend the canal. The passing centuries have blurred the edges of the earthworks, but enough remains to show how this worked. The canal here jinks sharply, so that the bastion stands in the angle of the corner. You will notice an area of flat land immediately you cross the canal. Between this flat land and the canal is a raised earthen bank. This was originally some 10 feet tall, masking the gun and its crew from the French on the far side of the canal. There is, however, a small section of much lower earthen bank barely two feet tall. It was through this gap that the British gun was trained to fire. If you look through the gap you will see that it offers a view directly along a lengthy straight stretch of canal. Any French soldiers trying to cross this section of the canal would have been exposed to fire from the British gun, as well as to musketry from defending soldiers. It was a deadly combination.

The return to Winchelsea takes the walk past the New Inn.

5) If you turn left at the lane you will find the entrance to the drive leading to Wickham Manor, which is not only a fine mansion but is also the home to a prestigious herd of organic lamb. Cuts of this delicious organic meat may be purchased here. Otherwise, at the lane turn right. After about 300 yards you will pass through New Gate, another of Edward I's defensive measures.

In the 13th century when the new town of Winchelsea was built on Hiham Hill the design of civic defences had reached a fine art. The hilltop was ringed by stone walls behind a dry ditch. The most vulnerable points of any defensive walls were the gates, which is why so much care was lavished on their design and construction. The gatehouses were much more solidly constructed than the walls, which is why they have survived while most of the walls have collapsed or been robbed of stone for local houses.

Winchelsea's old well is covered by a stone structure and was locked on Sundays.

Inside the walls stood the town of Winchelsea, but the defended area was not packed with houses. A fortified town such as this formed a key point in the nation's defences. When danger threatened the villagers from a wide area would flock to the town for protection, bringing with them their livestock, crops and anything of value that they could carry. Within the town walls there would have been open fields in which these refugees could camp and keep their animals while they sheltered from the enemy.

Even so the New Gate is surprisingly isolated. On the far side of it you will find pasture and open fields. Some of this area would have been open land even when Winchelsea was at the height of its prosperity, but not all of it. Archaeologists have been able to trace out the remains of streets and houses beneath the turf. The distance from New Gate to the buildings of Winchelsea that remain shows just how much this town has shrunk.

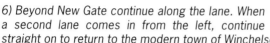

6) Beyond New Gate continue along the lane. When a second lane comes in from the left, continue **Climbing roses festoon a house in Winchelsea.**

straight on to return to the modern town of Winchelsea. You will find yourself entering the small town with the churchyard where the walk began on your right and the New Inn which serves lunch, tea and dinner, on your left.

Most of the town lies to the north of the church. There are a few shops and some lovely old houses, so feel free to explore if you wish. The 18th century New Inn offers much to the visitor. There is a large walled garden to be enjoyed during the summer months, and a cosy lounge with a roaring log fire for the winter. The chef makes a speciality of fresh, locally caught fish as well as hearty Sunday roasts.

An elaborate pediment tops a door to a house in Winchelsea.

Walk No. 12 Wisborough Green

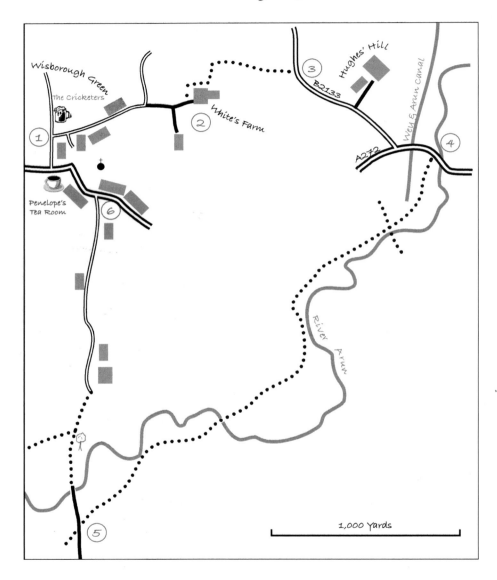

12 Wisborough Green 12/8/11

[handwritten note: No! Made us go on long busy road. Got lost in a field!]

Distance:	4.5 miles
Route:	Wisborough Green - Wisborough Green
Map:	OS Explorer 134
Teashop:	Penelope's Tea Room, Billingshurst Road, Wisborough Green.
Open:	Monday - Saturday 9 - 5; Sunday 9 - 4
Parking:	There is on-street parking in Wisborough Green.
Public Transport:	Wisborough Green is served by the Compass Travel bus route 76 from Billingshurst railway station.
Conditions:	This walk is mostly over unsurfaced paths and tracks, though two short sections run over roadside pavements. There are a couple of gentle slopes, but no difficult terrain.

This walk through the countryside around the pretty village of Wisborough Green runs alongside the Arun River as it meanders through its flood plain before striking south to carve its strategic gap in the South Downs. The southern end of the Wey and Arun Canal is crossed at one point, marking a small but significant piece of industrial heritage in this otherwise rural setting.

The Walk

1) Find your way to the extensive green that lies at the heart of the village. Much of the green is taken up by a cricket ground with a fine pavilion. The Cricketers pub stands on the east side of the green and offers good lunches. Leave the green heading east along the lane a little south of the pub. Where the lane bends sharp left, continue straight on along a surfaced track towards White's Farm.

2) Where this track bends sharp right, continue straight on again into White's Farm itself. Where the surfaced track opens out into the farmyard bear left and leave by way of a sturdy metal gate beside

The green at Wisborough Green is one of the largest in Sussex. A cricket ground and pavilion cover only part of the expanse of turf.

The aptly-named Cricketers pub overlooks the green at Wisborough Green.

which can be seen a Sussex County Council footpath sign. Follow this footpath north between fences. It then turns sharp right, again between fences, and strikes off across pasture fields.

3) The path eventually enters a small patch of woodland and crosses a stream by way of a wooden footbridge. Continue straight on through the woods to emerge onto the B2133.

This road is surprisingly busy for a B road, but there are wide grass verges to make walking alongside it for a stretch rather more pleasant. Turn right to walk south alongside the B2133 to the junction with the A272. Turn left. Almost immediately the road crosses a small bridge over first a canal and then a few yards further on a second bridge over a river.

The scene here is one of green fields, quiet waterways and tranquillity, but this spot was once one of the busiest inland ports in Britain. The River Arun runs from here south to enter the sea near Littlehampton. It had for centuries been used to bring goods inland as far as Pulborough, but in 1787 the river was deepened and widened as far as Billingshurst so that barges could reach that town. At much the same time the Wey had been improved as far as Godalming. There was a gap between the

The village sign at Wisborough Green takes the form of a striking monument erected in 1992.

two of barely 20 miles.

In 1813 the Earl of Egremont, who lived at Petworth, sponsored an Act of Parliament giving him permission to build a canal to link the navigable stretches of the Wey and the Arun. The advantages of such a canal were obvious. Not only would it link two already busy canals, but would link the upper Thames valley to the Channel. This in turn would provide a secure through-route for goods from the Midlands and from London. At this time Britain was at war with Napoleonic France and the narrow seas off Dover were notoriously rife with French

The walk leaves the farmyard of White's Farm by way of this stile beside a metal gate.

privateers and naval ships eager to snatch any unwary British merchant ship. Moving goods to Littlehampton by canal, then on by sea would be an undeniably safer route. Unfortunately for Egremont, but fortunately for everyone else, the wars were over by the time the canal was completed.

Despite this setback, the canal was an instant success. Barges plied back and forth, hauling up to 23,000 tons of goods each year. The demand for coal boomed creating the bulk of the heavy goods that were moved on the canal, but manufactured goods going in and out also played a role and as the 19th century Industrial Revolution gained pace so did the prosperity of the canal.

Horses graze the fields beside the footpath east of White's Farm.

Standing on the bridge and looking north you are gazing out over the site of the Newbridge Wharf. It was here that the Wey and Arun Canal left the Arun to strike northwest toward the Wey. There was a wharf here with warehouses and carthouses and stables. Dozens of men were employed here to shift goods, care for the horses that pulled both barge and cart and to maintain the barges. It was a bustling and busy part of the Industrial Revolution.

In 1865 a railway was built from Guildford to Horsham and within three years it had taken all the freight business away from the canal. In 1871 the canal closed completely. The stretches of the canal were sold off to the owners of the land through which it passed. Most of the canal became stretches of swampy, marshy water and mud. In 1970 a group of

As the path approaches the B2133 it passes this signpost then crosses a stream over a wooden footbridge to enter a small patch of woodland.

The Wey and Arun Canal at New Bridge lies stagnant and overgrown as it awaits renovation by the Trust that is working to restore the canal for leisure uses.

The Arun River south of New Bridge. The walk runs alongside the river for some distance.

enthusiasts formed the Wey and Arun Canal Trust with the aim of renovating the canal and returning it to use for pleasure boats. The Trust has achieved much, but sadly they have not yet reached this far south. One day they will.

For those interested in the canal, and who have the energy for a long distance trek, the Trust has marked out a path along the entire 23-mile length. Copies of a guide to the route can be obtained via the website http://www.weyandarun.co.uk.

4) Between the canal and the river a path leaves the road on the right by way of a metal gate. The path is signposted to Lording's Lock. The path runs through a short patch of woodland, then emerges onto the banks of the Arun. After following the river for some distance, the path peels off to the right to cut off a bend only to reach the river again and cross over it via a footbridge. Continue along the path until it meets a track.

5) Turn right to walk north along this track and recross the river by a more substantial bridge. Continue north along a path, passing a small wood on the right, until the path becomes a track once again. Continue north until the track meets the A272 at a T-junction.

6) Turn left along the A272. Just after the road takes a sharp left-hand bend there are a few shops on the left. One of these is Penelope's Tea Room.

Penelope herself is a charming and welcoming lady who is justly proud of her home-made cakes. She keeps a good range of these, plus an assortment of flapjacks, almond slices, scones and other individual baked treats. She will also make up sandwiches to order - there is usually a wide range of fresh fillings from which to choose - and salads are available as well. Unusually for a tea shop,

Penelope's is open for breakfast. A hearty meal of sausages, bacon, egg, mushroom and tomato is on offer for those customers who come this way before 11am. If you ask nicely she may cook breakfast at any time for someone hungry enough.

There is an outdoor seating area in front of the Tea Room for use in good weather, and ample seating inside the Tea Room. When you have rested your legs and eaten your fill, leave Penelope's Tea Room and bear left to return to the green where the walk began.

On its route back from the Arun River toward Wisborough Green the walk follows this surfaced lane.

Penelope's Tea Rooms are housed in what was once a shop.

The interior of Penelope's Tea Rooms are snug and cosy.

Walk No. 13   Jevington

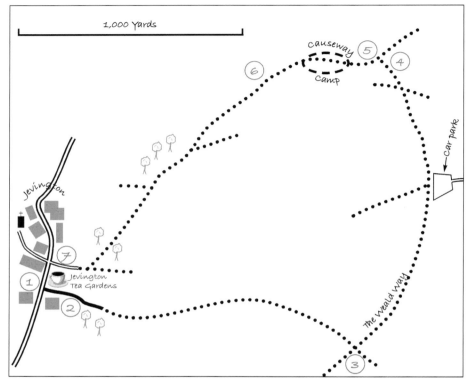

Beyond the trees the walk emerges onto open downland with grazing land on either side.

13 Jevington

Distance:	**3 miles**
Route:	**Jevington - Combe Hill - Jevington**
Map:	**OS Explorer 123**
Teashop:	**Jevington Tea Gardens, Jevington.**
Open:	**Tuesday to Sunday plus Bank Holiday Mondays 10 - 4.30**
Parking:	**There is a car park at the Jevington Tea Gardens and limited on-street parking in the village.**
Public Transport:	**Jevington is not served by bus routes and is not on the rail network.**
Conditions:	**This walk is mostly over unsurfaced paths. There is one demanding hill to be negotiated. The slopes are steep in places and the path surfaces uneven.**

A demanding walk in many senses of the word, this route offers magnificent views over the South Downs and north over the Pevensey Levels, former marshes that are now productive pastureland. The route passes prehistoric burial mounds and a causewayed enclosure, a Bronze Age structure of baffling purpose.

The Walk

1) There is only one road through Jevington, the lane that runs from Polegate to Friston. There is some limited on-street parking on this lane. The Jevington Tea Gardens lie toward the southern end of the village on the east side of the road. There is a small car park to the rear and - so long as you ask first - you should be welcome to park here while completing the walk and taking tea in the Tea Gardens afterward.

The Jevington Tea Gardens are truly delightful. As their name suggests there are lovely gardens to be enjoyed. In good weather tea can be taken in the gardens as there are plenty of garden tables and

The track that leaves Jevington Tea Gardens heading up towards the Downs passes between an avenue of trees for about 200 yards.

This stone stump marks the crossing point of the path with the Wealdway where the walk turns sharp left.

chairs on offer. In less clement weather tea can be taken in the large conservatory or the indoor lounge, both of which are remarkably comfortable.

The friendly and helpful staff have much to offer the hungry walker. There are home-made cakes, scones, teacakes and various other baked treats on offer as well as tea served in china and very hot. It is wise to take tea here early rather than later in the afternoon as the more popular cakes have a habit of being all eaten if the locals are out in force.

2) Leave the Jevington Tea Gardens by the car park entrance and turn left up a roughly surfaced track that runs beside the gardens. This track pushes through some woodland then degenerates into a footpath as it emerges onto the open Downs. The path runs between two fences with wide, sweeping, grazing fields on either side. The climb up the hill above Jevington is sustained and, in places, rather steep though it is not too arduous. There are plenty of opportunities to stop and gaze at the views while catching your breath.

The view east across Eastbourne toward Bexhill and Hastings.

3) This path eventually meets a second near the summit of the hill. This second path is the Wealdway, a long distance footpath that runs through Sussex. Turn left. Follow this path along the face of the hill toward a car park visible about half a mile away. At the car park ignore a path cutting off to the left down the slope back to Jevington which is now visible in the valley far below. Continue straight on through a gate and across the grassy Downs. After a short distance the path comes out onto the summit of the ridge, offering sweeping views to the north and east. On a clear day it is possible to see for miles across the Downs and the Weald.

4) Ignore a path that crosses the one you are on. Instead push on until the path meets another at T-junction beside a prehistoric burial mound, of a type generally called a barrow.

The Wealdway follows the crest of the ridge toward the car park about half a mile distant.

There are about 20,000 of these barrows spread across Britain. Some are highly elaborate, but most are similar to the one seen here. It is round and now rises to a height of about 8 feet, though it would originally have been rather taller. There is usually a single burial located underground near the centre of the barrow. Stones, some of them large, are often placed on top of the burial, then earth is dug up from a surrounding ditch and piled up to form the barrow. This is no mere mound of silt, however, the barrows are usually built up in layers of turf, chalk and rammed earth to make them more resilient to weathering.

A lone bench sits high on the downs looking toward Jevington.

The majority of round barrows date to the Bronze Age, about 1800 - 550BC. The people buried within them are presumed to be chiefs, kings or priests since they were clearly given much grander burials than the majority of people at the time. The grave goods buried with the men, or sometimes women, can be rich and impressive, but most often stretch only to food, drink and clothing.

The Bronze Age round barrow at which the walk turns left. Some chieftain or priest was buried here about 3,000 years ago.

5) In front of the barrow turn left and walk along the summit of this hill, Combe Hill. It is easy to miss the Causewayed Camp, but there is a ring of earthworks about halfway along the summit. The ditch and bank are now barely a foot tall, but if you look carefully you will see the ditch crossing the path about 75 yards from the barrow. There is a stretch of flat, smooth grassland after the ditch, then the path crosses the ditch again as it leaves the large circular enclosure.

This earthwork is of a type known to archaeologists as a Causewayed Camp or Causewayed Enclosure. These mysterious structures were built during the Neolithic or New Stone Age, making this structure as much as 2,000 years older than the barrow. There is only one ditch here, but other examples have as many as four. The ditches were never very deep, rarely more than three or four feet. At several places the ditches are broken by causeways of solid

The view north from Combe Hill toward Hailsham and the Weald.

The slight depression in the ground that marks the perimeter of the enigmatic causewayed camp that has stood on Combe Hill for about 5,000 years.

ground that cross them.

Archeological excavations have shown that these causewayed camps were never actually inhabited - no huts have been found within them. Nor were they carefully maintained. The ditches were allowed to silt up for years before they were dug out again and repaired. Only rarely are there burials in the enclosures, though there are often later barrows built nearby. Archaeologists have, however, found large quantities of cattle bones and other food waste.

It is something of a mystery what these structures were used for. They were clearly of some importance since the construction would have taken hundreds of man-hours of work. There are about 80 of them in Britain, 100 or so in France and another 100 or more in Belgium, Germany and Scandinavia.

The ditches are not large enough to have offered any meaningful defence to attack and the causeways would in any case make entrance easy. They do not mark out a settlement for there are no traces of buildings within them. Nor is it likely that they are linked to funerary practices as no graves are to be found.

Apart from the hoary old archeological standby explanation of "ritual purposes of some kind" that is

Beyond the causewayed camp the walk goes over this stile to begin the descent back down into Jevington.

The slope leading down to Jevington is covered in places by brambles. In the spring, as here, the bushes put forth delicate blossoms but in autumn they groan under the weight of blackberries.

so often employed to explain the inexplicable, there seem to be only a few ideas that might explain these ancient structures. The first is that they are cattle compounds into which livestock could be driven either to protect them from wolves or to prepare them for marking or slaughter. A second idea sees the enclosures as markets or trading centres. We know that trade was carried out over surprisingly long distances even 5,000 years ago. A network of tracks and paths linked places where particular

The final stretch down to Jevington village is across an open field leading to a lane between houses.

types of stone or other raw material were to be found. There is one at Ditchling, see Walk 9. Artefacts are sometimes found over a hundred miles from where they were produced.

However, the regular finds of cattle and sheep bones might indicate that the causewayed camps were used for feasting. This may have had a ritual or religious purpose or may have been to celebrate births, marriages and deaths among the local farming folk.

Whatever the camps were used for, they were clearly important to our ancestors. There is little to show it now up here on Combe Hill, but this was once a centre of great importance to the people who lived hereabouts.

6) Follow the path as it leaves the causewayed camp and passes a second Bronze Age barrow. The walk then crosses a stile before pushing on downhill across a broad grassy field. A path comes in from the left as the walk passes a small wood on the right. A short distance beyond the wood the path divides. Bear left to follow the path into a small but fairly dense wood. The slope becomes steeper here and the footing can be rough - and slippery in wet weather.

7) Beyond the wood the path crosses another stretch of grassy slope before going through a gate to join a short lane that runs down to the main street of Jevington. Emerging into the main street you will find a restaurant on your right. Straight ahead of you is a lane that leads to the parish church. Jevington Tea Gardens, where the walk began, are about 50 yards to the left.

The restaurant is a good one, though it does not serve afternoon tea. It is, however, world famous as being the place where an enterprising chef invented the dessert known as

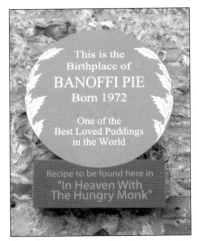

Few people know that Jevington has a claim to international fame. The sign says it all.

banoffi pie. They still serve it, lovingly prepared to the original recipe.

Jevington Church is one of several in Sussex dedicated to St Andrew. The tower was erected in about 920 or thereabouts and set into the inside of the nave wall is a sculpture which dates to around 950. The carving shows the resurrected Christ using a spear or long sword to stab a pair of writhing serpents at his feet. Presumably it symbolises the triumph of good over evil. Much of this early building uses Roman tiles and bricks taken from a nearby villa, now invisible above ground level.

The nave was built in Norman times, with the north aisle and chancel added soon after 1200. Rather than build a new chancel arch, the 13th century stonemasons took the old round-topped Norman arch, sliced off the top and added a pointy arch in the then fashionable Early English Gothic style. The resulting arch is a bit lopsided but has a charm not found in more elegant examples. A new roof was put on in about 1520 and is a magnificent example of Tudor Wagon Roof with hammer beams and king posts.

The path to the church is guarded by this golden lion, erected to mark the Silver Jubilee of Queen Elizabeth II.

Jevington's parish church is among the oldest in Sussex.

Walk No. 14 — Northiam

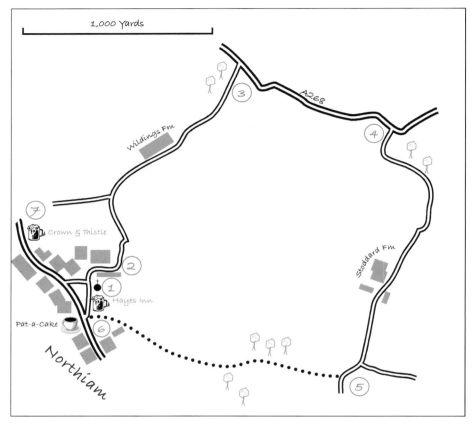

1,000 Yards

A268

Wildings Fm

Stoddard Fm

Crown & Thistle

Hayes Inn

Pat-a-Cake

Northiam

The Victorian chapel added to the parish church about 150 years ago has some of the finest stone carvings in the county.

14 Northiam

Distance:	**4 miles**
Route:	**Northiam - Northiam**
Map:	**OS Explorer 125**
Teashop:	**Pat-a-Cake Bakers & Tea Rooms, Main Street, Northiam.**
Open:	**Monday - Friday 8.30 - 4; Saturday 9 - 12.**
Parking:	**There is a small car park and ample on-street parking in Northiam.**
Public Transport:	**Northiam is served by Coastal Coaches Buses 340 and 344 from central Hastings.**
Conditions:	**The walk is largely over quiet lanes, but one lengthy stretch is across open fields that can be muddy after rain. There are no steep hills and no difficult terrain.**

Northiam has every appearance of being a fairly sleepy little village, and in many ways it is. The houses are clustered around the church and village green while gently rolling countryside spreads out on all sides. But that is not to say that nothing has ever happened here.

The Walk

1) Find your way to the parish church that lies just to the east of the main road through the village.

A church stood here in about 900, probably it was made of wood, but the oldest surviving parts of the structure are the lower sections of the tower and nave walls that date to around 1080. This church was enlarged by the addition of aisles in around 1320 and the upper sections of the tower and the spire were added around 1480. In 1845 the chancel was enlarged and the imposing Frewen Chapel built on the church's western side. The exterior of the chapel is graced by numerous carvings and inscriptions, while the inside holds the tombs and monuments of the Frewen family, a local landowning dynasty that still resides nearby.

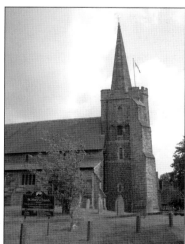

The walk starts at the parish church in Northiam, which is worth a visit for its fine stained-glass windows.

As it leaves the village the walk passes along a quiet lane lined by towering banks and hedges.

A corbel carving beside the door to the church.

The interior of the church is famous for its carved oak panelling and pulpit plus the brass candelabra in the chancel. However, altogether more charming is the little stained-glass window in the east aisle which shows the Nativity of Christ firmly set in a beautifully depicted Sussex farmyard.

2) Leave the churchyard through the iron gates and turn right along the lane. This lane turns first right, then left as it leaves the village. It then plunges down a slope between high hedged banks before passing a lane on the left and emerging into more open fields by Wildings Farm. Continue along the lane until it ends at a T-junction with the A268.

3) At the T-junction turn right. There are wide grass verges on which to walk beside the A road.

4) Take the first turning on the right, a lane signposted to Clayhill. Continue along this lane as it twists and turns over the gentle hills to pass Stoddard Farm with its twin oasthouses. Where a lane joins from the left, bear right.

5) A few yards further on the lane bends sharply left. A footpath continues straight on over a stile and along an avenue of trees. Take this footpath, running along the edge of a grass field before entering a small wood and crossing a stream by way of a footbridge. Follow the footpath until it emerges between houses onto the A28 Main Street in the centre of Northiam. On the far side of the road and slightly to your right you will see the Pat-a-Cake Bakers & Tea Rooms.

Delicately shaded wild roses festoon the hedgerows on the lane around Wildings Farm.

This teashop is as much a bakery of quality breads and cakes as it is a teashop. On entering the counter for bakery dominates the scene, the tables and chairs of the tea room being round a corner to the right. All the tempting delights on offer in the bakery can be eaten in the tea room,

The distinctive twin oasthouses of Stoddard Farm on the lane leading back towards Northiam.

including a bread pudding that is deliciously light and has become famous among the locals. There are also sandwiches, savouries and soups on offer. A full English breakfast is served until 11am. And if you are taking tea alone there is a fine array of reading matter for you to borrow.

6) Leaving the Pat-a-Cake Bakers & Tea Rooms you will see the village green spreading out to your left on the other side of the main road. The Hayes Inn stands on the far side of the green. It serves delicious lunches and tea.

Dominating the green are two unusual structures. The first is the old village pump, housed in a roofed structure to protect it from the elements. The second is a massive tree stump to which is affixed a metal plate.

On 11th August 1573 Queen Elizabeth I was travelling from London to Rye when her coach pulled up here for the Queen and her entourage to have a picnic breakfast served from the Hayes Inn. It was a hot sunny day, so Good Queen Bess sat on the grass in the shade of what was then a vastly spreading oak tree. Her shoes were obviously troubling her, so she took them off and presented them to the woman in charge of the Hayes Inn by way of thanks for her attentive service. The shoes survive more than four centuries later. They are made of green damask silk, have pointed toes and heels 2.5 inches high.

A traditional wooden finger signpost gives the names of the lanes. The walk continues along Church Lane.

The walk abandons the lane to go over this stile and along an avenue of trees toward Northiam.

7) Having inspected the historic tree stump, walk north along Main Street to find the Crown and Thistle pub and adjacent playing fields.

On 12th May 1944 Northiam again played a minor role in history when Winston Churchill came here to confer with the Prime Ministers of Canada, South Africa and Rhodesia. The subject for discussion was the imminent D-Day invasion of occupied Europe. The invasion was to involve hundreds of ships, thousands of aircraft and hundreds of thousands of troops drawn from the British Empire and the USA. The four prime ministers met to discuss the details of the landings and how men from their respective countries would be involved. After the meeting a parade was held on the playing fields outside the pub.

Return back along Main Street, turning left up Church Lane to return to the church where the walk began and now ends.

The battered tree stump, all that remains of the massive oak tree beneath which Queen Elizabeth I rested on her visit to Northiam.

The comfortable lounge at Pat-a-Cake Bakers & Tea Rooms offers a refreshing cup of tea to thirsty walkers.

Pat-a-Cake is housed in a single-storey building squeezed between taller houses in Main Street facing the green.

Winston Churchill paid a secretive visit to Northiam only a few days before the D-Day invasion of France in 1944.

The village pump at Northiam is protected by a fine wooden canopy.

A fine carving of St George tops the war memorial at Northiam.

Walk No. 15   Rottingdean

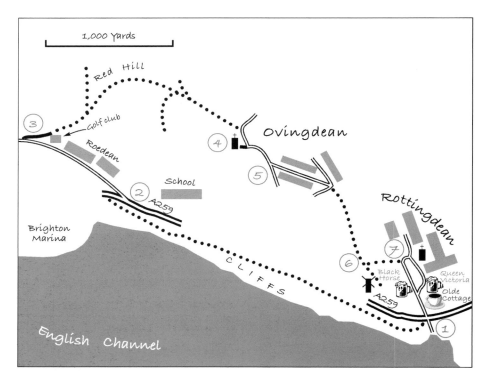

A view down into Brighton Marina from the footpath beside the A259.

15 Rottingdean

Distance:	**5 miles**
Route:	**Rottingdean - Ovingdean - Roedean - Rottingdean**
Map:	**OS Explorer 122**
Teashop:	**The Olde Cottage Tea Rooms, 62 High Street, Rottingdean.**
Open:	**Monday - Saturday 10 - 4.30**
Parking:	**There is a car park in Rottingdean and some very limited on-street parking.**
Public Transport:	**Rottingdean is served by various routes of the Brighton & Hove Bus and Coach Company Bus from Brighton.**
Conditions:	**This walk goes over the South Downs west of the village. There is a fairly stiff climb up to the hills, but once there the going is easier. The paths over the chalk turf are firm underfoot and well drained.**

This reasonably stiff walk takes in three downland villages to the east of Brighton and gives a good idea of what that bustling resort was like when it was the humble fishing village of Brighthelmstone. The village of Rottingdean was the scene of a murderous raid by the French during the Hundred Years War, the marks of which can still be seen. Roedean is better known for its private school, which can be seen but not visited on this walk.

The Walk

1) In Rottingdean make your way to the small seafront and beach. Walk north to the A259 and turn left. Almost immediately join the footpath that veers off to the left to follow the seafront. This path climbs steadily, but not steeply as the ground rises. The beach on the left is replaced by sheer cliffs that eventually reach a height of around 130 feet. The path does not stray far from the A259, but is far enough away to be a peaceful route.

The buildings of the famous girls' school dominate the hills above Roedean.

The path from the golf club up to Red Hill is wide and well surfaced.

To the right can be seen the towering mass of Roedean School. The school was founded in 1885 as a school for young ladies by three sisters: Penelope, Millicent, and Dorothy Lawrence. The school has gone from strength to strength and is now recognised as being one of the foremost girls' schools in Britain. The buildings are impressive, but not open to the public.

2) Beyond the school the path rejoins the A259 just as that road becomes a dual carriageway. Turn right, then cross the main road with care to join a lane cutting up the hill towards the group of houses that is Roedean village.

3) Pass Roedean. The road goes through a sunken section, then a drive leading to a golf club cuts back to the right. Follow this drive to the golf club, then continue straight on along a surfaced footpath that runs up the shoulder of Red Hill to the northeast. This hill gives magnificent views over Brighton to the west.

4) Continue up and over the summit of the hill, then continue along the footpath down the other side to emerge into the village of Ovingdean beside the church.

The pretty little church at Ovingdean is usually kept locked, which is a shame, but if it is open it is worth a visit.

5) Continue past the church, then take the first road on the left lined by houses to climb a slope. At the top of the slope the road ends. Continue on along a footpath signposted as heading for Rottingdean.

6) Continue along the footpath until about 150 yards before the famous Rottingdean windmill. Turn left down a second footpath that runs down the slope into Rottingdean itself,

The view down to Brighton from Red Hill. Several famous buildings can be picked out from the hilltop.

Ovingdean church is set back from the village high street in its crowded churchyard.

now visible in the valley below.

Wildflowers cover a grave in Ovingdean churchyard.

The Rottingdean Windmill was originally a flour mill, but gained its initial fame as a landmark for ships using the English Channel. Its distinctive appearance and prominent position made it unmistakable. By the early 20th century it was no longer needed for flour milling and fell into decay. In 1922 it was fully restored and is today maintained as a landmark by the local council. One local resident, Sir William Nicholson, was so fond of the windmill that he used it as the logo for his company, the famous Nicholson publishing house.

7) *The footpath emerges between houses onto a lane. Turn right to find the village green. Continue straight over the green into High Street. The Olde Cottage Tea Rooms are on your left.*

Rottingdean and its green appear peaceful nowadays, but it was not always thus. One grim day in June 1377 a fleet of more than 40 ships appeared off the beach at Rottingdean. Knowing trouble when they saw it, the villagers fled inland as fast as their feet would

The path from Ovingdean to Rottingdean strikes out across the bare open grassland of the Downs.

carry them. They had good reason to run for England was at war with France and the ships flew the French flag. The commander of the fleet was a Spanish mercenary named Don Fernao Sanchez de Tovar. He and his men had already burned Rye (see walk 16) and been thrown back by the defences of Winchelsea. They were after loot and pillage.

As the French and Spaniards swarmed ashore, one Rottingdean villager was riding hard for Lewes where the local militia were gathered. Led by John de Caroloco, Prior of Lewes, supported by two local knights Sir John Falvesley and Sir Thomas Cheyne, the militia at once set out for Rottingdean to confront the invaders. Sadly the English thought that only around 300 Frenchmen had come ashore whereas in fact about a 1,000 had landed. The

The windmill above Rottingdean. The walk turns left just before reaching this famous landmark.

Rottingdean seen from the hills to the west over which the walk approaches the village on its return from Roedean.

The Old Cottage Tea Rooms in Rottingdean's High Street stands between the green and the sea.

500 English militia were therefore heavily outnumbered.

John de Caroloco did not realise his mistake until he marched into Rottingdean and was ambushed by the invaders. The fight was short and sharp, but the end result was never really in doubt. About a hundred Englishmen were killed on and around the green. John de Caroloco and Sir Thomas Cheyne were both captured, Sir John Falvesley managed to make his escape along with a hundred or so others. The French then burned Rottingdean, looted the surrounding area thoroughly and left a few days later.

The church was rebuilt after the raid, though the scorch marks of the burning can still be seen on some of the reused stones. The original Norman font remains from the original church. Rather more recent are the beautiful stained-glass windows by Edward Burne-Jones. Early in the 20th century the Church of England received an offer to buy this church. The offer came from the council of Los Angeles, California, which was then constructing Forest Lawns Cemetery. They seem to have been struck by the beauty of the church and by its links to the poet Rudyard Kipling, who lived in Rottingdean for some years and wrote his poem *Recessional* while here. The Church of England turned down the offer, but did allow the Americans to survey and photograph the building so that they could build a precise replica in California.

The Olde Cottage Tea Rooms are a charming old venue for taking afternoon tea, and offer a bewildering array of treats. There is not only a good Indian tea on the menu, but also Earl Grey, Lapsang Souchong, Darjeeling, Lady Grey, Assam and Ceylon. Nor does the variety end with the teas. There are scones (served with cream or butter), cakes (lemon curd, lime drizzle, coffee and walnut, chocolate fudge and Victoria sandwich), pastries, sandwiches, toasted tea cakes, apple crumble and

The Californian government once made an offer to buy Rottingdean Church, but settled for making a copy instead.

assorted snacks. The Olde Cottage also serves cooked breakfasts until 11am and a variety of luncheon dishes. The Black Horse and the Queen Victoria pubs in the High Street both serve good lunches and pots of tea.

Leave the tea rooms and turn left to return to the start of the walk.

The green at Rottingdean was the scene of a murderous battle during the Hundred Years War between England and France.

Walk No. 16

Rye

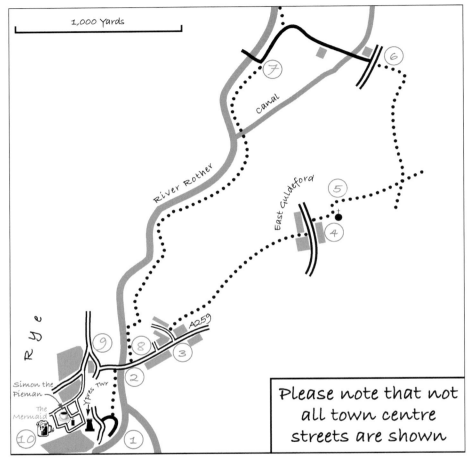

1,000 Yards

canal

River Rother

East Guldeford

A259

R y e

Ypres Twr

Simon the Pieman

The Mermaid

Please note that not all town centre streets are shown

The old town stocks stand outside the Ypres Tower which served as the town prison once it was no longer needed for defensive purposes.

16 Rye

Distance:	**3.8 miles**
Route:	**Rye - East Guldeford - Rye**
Map:	**OS Explorer 125**
Teashop:	**Simon the Pieman Bakery and Tea Rooms, Lion Street, Rye.**
Open:	**Monday to Saturday 9.30 - 4.30; Sunday 1.30 - 5**
Parking:	**There are car parks in Rye.**
Public Transport:	**Rye is served by the railway.**
Conditions:	**The walk starts in the hilltop town of Rye, then drops down to the banks of the River Rother and surrounding farmland. The unsurfaced paths over the farmland can be muddy in wet weather and the climb to and from Rye town centre is short, but steep.**

The historic town of Rye is one of the Cinque Ports, the five ports that dominated the medieval wool trade with the Continent. It grew rich on the trade though this made it a target for both pirates and the king's enemies. The harbour silted up in the 16th century, though Rye retained importance as a centre for the lush farmland that surrounds it. This walk takes in the more historic buildings in Rye itself before pushing out onto the scenic farmlands to the northeast.

The Walk

1) In Rye find the Ypres Tower, which is well signposted.

This sturdy fortress was built in 1249 as a key element in the defences of this hilltop town. At the time Rye was a bustling and thriving port at the mouth of the River Rother. The harbour stood at the foot of the hill directly beneath Ypres Tower. The harbour was then much larger than now, encompassing a large area of what is now flat pastureland.

Rye's Ypres Tower seen from the artillery bastion beneath. The walk starts at this ancient tower that houses the town museum.

Rye enjoyed a great degree of freedom from royal government at the time - a fact of which the local merchants took full advantage. The town, along with Winchelsea (see Walk 11) was an Ancient Town within the confederacy of the Cinque Ports. The Cinque Ports themselves being Hastings, Dover, Sandwich, Hythe and New Romney. In return for providing the king with ships and the men to sail them in times of war, the towns were exempt from taxation and were free to administer their own courts and justice system. The Cinque Ports system dated to at least 1151 and by the 1240s when this tower was built had become the premier merchant and shipping concern in England.

The walk leaves the old town by descending a flight of stone steps past the Ypres Inn, which offers tasty lunches and well-kept real ales.

The town was attacked by the French four times. It held out on three occasions but in 1377 was captured and burned. The Ypres Tower was one of the few structures to survive. The introduction of artillery and gunpowder rendered the stone town walls and Ypres Tower redundant as defences. The building later served as a court, a jail and a private house. It now houses Rye Museum which has hundreds of exhibits and interactive displays about the local area.

Down the flight of stone steps and through an arch to the south of the tower is a broad artillery bastion constructed to bolster the defences of the town in Tudor times. On this platform were mounted cannon to guard the harbour below. The guns there today are rather later, dating to the 18th and early 19th centuries.

All that is left of the once thriving port of Rye is this tidal wharf for fishing boats at the foot of the hill on which the old town stands.

2) Having explored Ypres Tower and the bastion, take the footpath running east in front of the Ypres Tower. This goes down a steep flight of steps, passing the Ypres Tower public house which serves good lunches, to reach the modern ring road that circles the old town at the foot of the hill. Cross this road with care, heading straight on along a narrow lane leading to an industrial estate. Near the end of this lane turn left along a footpath that runs beside playing fields and a public park. At the end of this footpath turn right alongside the A259 to cross the River Rother.

The walk passes through this gate to strike off across the fields toward East Guldeford.

East Guldeford Church is an unusual Tudor construction which is famed for its magnificent interior woodwork.

Look to your right as you cross the river to see what remains of Rye Harbour. These days there is simply a wharf along a bend in the tidal river. Fishing boats tie up here. When the boats have come in it is possible to buy fish and seafood straight off the wharf, a small sign is displayed on the Rye side of the bridge when fish are for sale. The harbour began silting up around 1450 and by 1550 the problem was becoming too much for the small scale dredging tools then available. By 1600 Rye had ceased to be a harbour of any real mercantile importance. However, the town itself was by then an important centre for the surrounding farmland, so its prosperity was assured. The odd bit of smuggling also went on and by the 18th century had become a fairly major industry in its own right. As many as 300 men were thought to earn their living primarily through smuggling at one time.

3) Once over the bridge continue along the A259 past a small housing development and take the second turning on the left. After about 30 yards a footpath leaves this road to the right signposted to East Guldeford.

4) Follow this path over damp pasture land to emerge back on to the A259 in the middle of that small village. Turn left, then almost immediately right along a second footpath signposted to East Guldeford Church.

This humble church is usually locked, but a key is

The route across the otherwise featureless damp pastureland beyond East Guldeford is marked by these small plastic signs on the occasional wooden post.

Crossing the railway line is by way of this wooden platform. Great care should be taken as the trains travel this stretch of line at some speed.

The path along the bank of the Rother heading back to Rye is clearly defined and well-maintained.

available from one of the cottages in the village. Services are held here regularly, though only once per month. The brick structure was put up in 1505 by the local landowner Sir Richard Guldeford. The marshes and swamps were then being drained to produce pasture land and the local population was rising fast, and a new place of worship was needed. The church is a simple rectangle with a double pitched roof and a small belfry. It is worth borrowing the key as the interior is filled with elegant box pews. These are a rare survival as the Victorians swept them away in most churches. There is also an elaborate three-decker pulpit, another rarity.

The walk re-enters the old town of Rye through this medieval gateway.

5) Turn left just in front of the church and cross a drainage ditch by way of a narrow footbridge. Beyond the bridge turn sharp right and set off across the flat, damp meadows that now occupy the land that was once marsh, swamp and bog. There are numerous ditches to be crossed and fences to be negotiated by stile or gate. The way is marked by small plastic blue arrows affixed to upright posts. It is best to try to locate the next post by looking in the direction indicated by the arrow before setting off. After about 300 yards a second path crosses the first, running in a north/south direction. Turn left to head north toward a railway embankment visible about 700 yards distant. Again follow the blue arrows on posts.

6) The path eventually reaches a stile, which gives access to a pedestrian crossing over the railway. Cross with care. A second stile then takes the walk into a field beyond which is the A259. Cross the A259 and head down a narrow surfaced lane past some farm buildings and over a bridge that crosses a major drainage channel akin to a canal. The

track continues on, turning left where it meets the River Rother.

7) Immediately before the track turns right and crosses the River Rother by way of a bridge a footpath goes straight on. This is a section of the Sussex Border Path and is both well signed and reasonably surfaced. Take this path and follow the banks of the Rother to emerge on to the A259 beside the bridge by which you left Rye at Point 2 in the walk.

8) Turn right. Cross the bridge and follow the A259 to a T-junction. Turn right, then take the first left that cuts back toward the old town.

9) Where this lane bends right continue straight on through the Town Gate. This lane bends right to become the High Street. The second on the left is Lion Street, which has the parish church visible at its far end. Turn up Lion Street to find Simon the Pieman Bakery and Tea Rooms near the top on the left.

The Old Grammar School is just one of many historic buildings in Rye's High Street.

Simon the Pieman is a shop of two halves. The right hand entrance leads into the bakery section where mouth-watering selections of cakes, breads and pastries are for sale. The left-hand door leads to the teashop where those same delicacies can be ordered and consumed alongside a nice fresh pot of tea. The quaint lounge makes an ideal place to enjoy a good, traditional afternoon tea.

10) Leaving the tea rooms, turn right to walk past the birthplace of Tudor playwright John Fletcher. Just in front of the church turn right along a path that comes out in front of Lamb House. Turn right then immediately left into Mermaid Street to find The Mermaid Hotel on the right hand side about 50 yards along. Retrace your steps to Lamb House then skirt the edge of the churchyard to return to Ypres Tower where the walk began.

Lamb House is owned by the National Trust and is open to the public. It was home to the

American novelist Henry James for some 40 years after he moved here in 1876. It was here that James produced some of his finest novels and short stories. He habitually wrote in a summer house in the garden - which was unfortunately destroyed by a German bomb in 1940.

The Mermaid Hotel is one of the finest and most historic buildings in Rye - and a jolly good hotel as well. Quite how old the building might be is not entirely clear. It is most likely of 15th century origin, though it has been altered and changed numerous times since

The Simon the Pieman stands near the top of Lion Street.

Rye's Simon the Pieman offers a tempting and rather impressive array of cakes, pastries, biscuits and other treats to the walker.

and only parts of it are that old. In the 18th century this was a favoured haunt of the notorious Hawkhurst Gang of smugglers. These were vicious and deadly criminals who thought nothing of slitting throats of informers. They dominated the smuggling trade in this area for some years before they were finally brought to justice.

Rye's parish church, dedicated to St Mary, was built in around 1150. Not much of that original church survived the French raid of 1377, though some walls do remain. Most of what is to be seen today dates from the rebuilding of Rye after the raid and to a major Victorian renovation. The interior is famed for its 18th century mahogany carvings and Victorian stained glass. The tower houses a clock made in 1560 and is the oldest church clock in England still with its original mechanism. The tower is sometimes open to the public and, in good weather, gives stunning views over the surrounding countryside.

The comfortable interior of Simon the Pieman is found by using the left hand door in the facade.

Rye's Mermaid Hotel was once a haunt of a notorious and violent gang of smugglers.

Lamb House, where novelist Henry James produced some of his most famous works.

Rye's church has what might be the oldest clock in Sussex.

Walk No. 17

Seaford

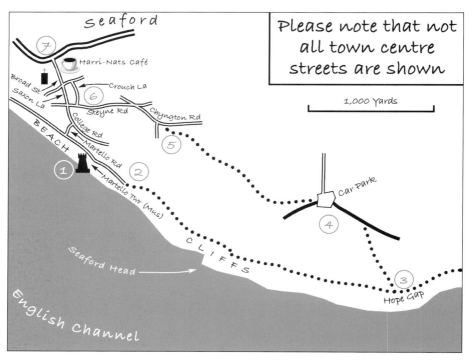

Seaford

Harri-Nats Café

Broad St
Saxon La

Crouch La

Steyne Rd

Chyngton Rd

College Rd

Martello Rd

Martello Twr (Mus)

BEACH

CLIFFS

Seaford Head

English Channel

Car Park

Hope Gap

Please note that not all town centre streets are shown

1,000 Yards

The Seaford walk starts at the old Martello tower which houses the town museum and has a free car park.

17 Seaford

Distance:	**5 miles**
Route:	**Seaford - Seaford Head - Seaford**
Map:	**OS Explorer 123**
Teashop:	**Harri-Nats, 30 Broad Street, Seaford.**
Open:	**Monday - Saturday 9.30 - 4.30**
Parking:	**There is a car park beside the Seaford Museum where the walk starts and ends.**
Public Transport:	**Seaford is served by the railway.**
Conditions:	**This walk is mostly over unsurfaced paths over the chalk turf of the South Downs to the east of Seaford itself. There is one hill to be climbed, which is high but not especially steep.**

This hill top walk begins on the edge of Seaford, takes in a nearby hill with one of the most famous views in England and then returns to the town. Seaford was one of the busiest small ports on the South Coast until 1579 when extensive floods during a storm caused the River Ouse to alter its course to the west. Seaford port was left literally high and dry overnight to be revived only in Victorian times as a smaller seaside resort. The walk takes in a stretch of the scenic Sussex Heritage Coast.

The Walk

1) Find your way to the Seaford Museum, housed in a Martello Tower on the beach towards the southern edge of town. The museum is signposted from the railway station and from the town centre.

This museum is open Wednesday to Sunday in the summer, but during the winter months on Sundays and Bank Holiday Mondays only. It is well worth a visit not only to see the impressive array of exhibits, but also to walk around the inside of a Martello Tower. These coastal forts were built between 1805 and 1812 to guard the south and eastern coasts from attack by the French of the Emperor Napoleon. The

The extensive shingle beach at Seaford is lined by colourful beach huts.

Boats are pulled up onto the beach at Seaford.

towers took their name and design from the Torre di Martello in Corsica which fought off a British frigate in 1793.

Although the main impetus behind the construction of the 103 Martello Towers was the fear of a French invasion, they were also a key component in the guarding of coastal merchant trade against sudden attacks by French ships. Each fort was garrisoned by 23 men and one officer who lived and worked inside the 13 foot thick walls. Each fort had a single 24-pound gun mounted on the roof that was able to traverse through a full 360 degrees on a complex sliding carriage. The guns were able to fire inland to guard against parties of Frenchmen landing and trying to attack from the rear. Each Martello also had a small furnace in which the cannon balls could be heated until they became white hot. When fired at wooden ships, this heated shot was capable of starting a fire that could consume even the largest warship in minutes.

Most Martellos saw action only against a few French privateers or naval raiders as Napoleon never did invade Britain. Of the 103 built about 43 survive more or less intact. This one is more intact than most and even has its gun in situ. There is a small kiosk serving teas and cakes at the museum although seating is limited.

2) From the Martello Tower walk southeast along the Promenade to the end of Seaford's shingle beach. Where the Promenade ends the footpath up Seaford Head begins. Follow this path up the grassy slope in front of you to keep the cliffs on your right. This is a windy area and can be blustery when only a breeze is wafting through Seaford itself.

The summit of the hill is occupied by a semi-circular earthwork. This almost certainly dates

The towering heights of Seaford Head dominate the eastern end of the beach. The walk climbs up and over this hill.

The view along the Seven Sisters cliffs toward Beachy Head is one of the finest in Sussex.

back to pre-Roman times and formed a fortified refuge for the Celtic farmers who lived in the surrounding area. Whether the defences were ever put to a military test we do not know. Certainly the Romans did not attack as this area welcomed the invasion as the chance to throw off the onerous rule of another Celtic tribe - see walk 6 Fishbourne. To the east of the earthwork is a modern beacon in which a fire was lit to celebrate the Silver Jubilee of Queen Elizabeth II in 1977.

3) Pass over the crest of the hill and then descend down to Hope Gap. At Hope Gap there is a break in the cliffs where a combe runs down to a tiny beach. There is a notice board here giving details about the Seaford Head Nature Reserve, and the plants and animals that can be found here. Turn left here to follow a path up the combe to the northwest. As you climb out of the combe look to your right to see the magnificent chalk cliffs of the Seven Sisters with the towering bulk of Beachy Head in the distance. This dramatic and impressive coastline is one of the most famous in southern England.

4) Where the path joins a track, turn left to reach a car park and old barn. On the far side of the car park ignore the surfaced track that runs off to the beacon. Instead head almost directly west along a footpath. This crosses the Seaford Head golf course as it goes downhill.

The path up the combe from Hope Gap toward the hilltop.

5) Where the footpath meets a road bear left along Chyngton Road. At a crossroads turn left down Steyne Road.

6) At another crossroads turn right into Saxon Lane that becomes Broad Street, the main shopping street of Seaford.

Harri-Nats is part shop, part tea room. It stands on the right side of Broad Street near the northern end of the street on the junction with Sutton Road. Harri-Nats offers a selection of teas, plus some herbal brews, as well as coffees. The baked delicacies are truly impressive with buns, teacakes, cakes, scones and much more, always freshly baked and temptingly on offer. Sandwiches and salads are also on offer, as are jacket potatoes. Nobody need go hungry at Harri-Nats.

7) Having taken tea, return down Broad Street and Saxon Lane then cross over Steyne Road into College Road. Turn right along Martello Road to reach the beach. Turn left to return to the museum where the walk began. Alternatively continue along seafront to the Beachcomber pub which is open on Sundays.

Harri-Nats serves fresh tea and tasty cakes to shoppers in Seaford's bustling town centre.

Walk No. 18 — Tangmere

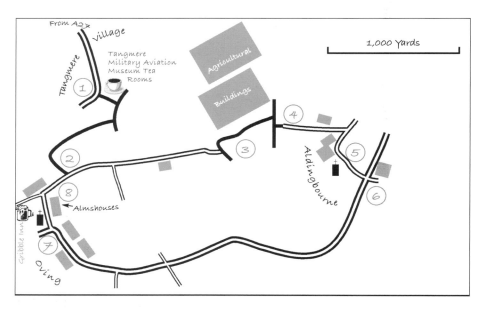

The entrance to the Tangmere Military Aviation Museum where the walk begins and ends.

18 Tangmere

Distance:	**5 miles**
Route:	**Tangmere - Oving - Aldingbourne - Tangmere**
Map:	**OS Explorer 120**
Teashop:	**Tangmere Aviation Museum Teashop**
Open:	**Daily 10 - 4**
Parking:	**There is a car park at Tangmere Aviation Museum.**
Public Transport:	**Tangmere is served by Stagecoach bus route 55 from central Chichester.**
Conditions:	**This walk is mostly over country lanes with some sections across the surfaced paths and tracks of the old RAF Tangmere fighter station.**

This gentle stroll takes the walker across what used to be the Tangmere RAF base that served as one of the main centres for Fighter Command during the Battle of Britain. Douglas Bader, Johnnie Johnson and other fighter aces flew from here to protect Britain from invasion by the Germans in 1940. Later, in 1944, many of the air missions connected to the D-Day landings in Normandy also flew from here. Today the RAF base has been largely returned to farmland, with industrial concerns occupying the old buildings. There is a fine museum dedicated to the RAF days, at which this walk starts and finishes.

The Walk

1) Find The Tangmere Military Aviation Museum which stands at the southern end of Tangmere village off the road to Shopwhyke. The museum is signposted from the A27 east of Chichester.

The museum was founded in 1982 by a group of local enthusiasts when the RAF base here closed down. Much of the museum is devoted to the history of RAF Tangmere, but there is much else besides. There is a Spitfire and a Hurricane, recalling the heroic days of the Battle of Britain, a Meteor and a Hunter that held world air speed

The pilots of No.601 Fighter Squadron of the RAF photographed at Tangmere in 1940 at the height of the Battle of Britain.

A squadron of Hurricanes flies high over Sussex in 1940. During the Battle of Britain Tangmere was a Hurricane base.

records when flying from here and a Lightning that introduced supersonic combat to the RAF. Visitors can try their skills at a flight simulator, sit in the cockpits of historic aircraft and generally

The famous ace Douglas Bader stands on his Hurricane at Tangmere at the time he commanded the base in the summer of 1941.

revel in the atmosphere of military aviation. There are thousands of exhibits in all. The tea room stands to the left of the main entrance and serves a tempting range of hot drinks, cakes and snacks.

2) From the museum bear left along an old track to pass through a gateway. The track then meets a second at a T-junction. Turn right, then turn right again after barely 50 yards. Follow this track over open fields for some distance. After bending left the track emerges on to a lane. Turn left and follow this lane for almost a mile until it ends at a gateway that gives access to a wide expanse of concrete. This is the old taxiway of RAF Tangmere built to take the heavy weight of jet fighters in the post-war period.

3) Turn left and follow the taxiway as it bends right and heads east with large agricultural buildings on your left. At a T-junction with another taxiway turn right.

This whole area once formed RAF Tangmere, one of the main fighter bases of the Royal Air Force for decades. The buildings of the base were either demolished or converted for

business use after the base closed in 1967. The runway is still there, behind the agricultural buildings and now not open to the public, as is the control tower and other buildings. To the south of the taxiway can be seen the massive concrete blast walls that were installed in the 1950s. They were partly to protect aircraft parked beside them from bomb blasts and partly to deaden the deafening roar of the jet engines then in use.

A Spitfire MkI cruises over Sussex in the summer of 1941. Bader was flying one of these aircraft when he was shot down and captured over France that year.

RAF Tangmere began life in 1916 when a pilot experienced engine trouble and

A Spitfire MkV tears through the skies in the summer of 1943. By this date the pilots flying out of Tangmere were carrying the fight into enemy skies over France on a regular basis.

landed on a field south of the village. His report caught the eye of a senior officer who was looking for an area of flat land near the south coast for use as an airfield for the Royal Flying Corps (RFC). The base was quickly in operation training pilots for combat over the trenches in France and providing a staging post for aircraft flying out to France. When the RFC was merged into the new RAF in 1918, the Tangmere base transferred with it.

Throughout the 1920s and 1930s, RAF Tangmere remained little more than a collection of wooden buildings and a grass runway. Then, in 1938, the RAF ordered a massive redevelopment as Tangmere was earmarked to be one of the main bases for 11 Group of RAF Fighter Command, tasked with protecting the naval base of Portsmouth and the docks of Southampton from air attack. In 1938 two squadrons of modern Hurricane fighters moved in and Tangmere became a fully operational combat base. It was none to soon for war broke out in 1939.

At first Tangmere was rather a second line station. The few German bombers that did attack Britain came in off the North Sea putting Kent and East Anglia in the front line. But when France fell in June 1940 the German Luftwaffe acquired a host of new bases along the northern French coast. Tangmere was now in the thick of things. As the Battle of Britain developed, Tangmere increased in size and importance. By July 1940 there were four squadrons on the base, more aircraft were based at the satellite airfield at Westhampnett a few miles to the west. The Sector Operations Room in Tangmere controlled all fighter squadrons over Sussex vectoring them in by radio on the vast German formations thundering over the Channel to attack Britain.

The pace of combat increased steadily as the Germans attacked first coastal convoys, then turned their attentions to airfields and radar stations. On 13th August the Luftwaffe chief Hermann Goering unleashed his massed squadrons in an operation he dubbed Adlertag - "Eagle Day". The morning raids were on Kent, but in the afternoon it was Tangmere's turn. Hundreds of German aircraft headed for Portsmouth and Southampton, and the pilots out

of Tangmere went up to meet them. Four Hurricanes were shot down, but the Tangmere pilots accounted for a dozen raiders.

Next day Tangmere itself was attacked. A horde of Stuka divebombers raced in over the coast then swooped down to pound the airfield. Where you are now standing was then the dispersal area where fighters were parked for refuelling and rearming. This took the brunt of the first wave with bombs falling all about, blasting the area with

The walk passes through this fence to reach a lane after crossing fields south of the museum.

A section of taxiway that survives from the days that this was an RAF fighter base. The walk passes the length of this stretch of tarmac.

high explosive and shrapnel. Anyone standing here would have been killed instantly. Fortunately all the ground crew had got into bomb shelters, but seven aircraft were destroyed on the ground. The second wave hit the hangars, destroying one and setting another on fire - along with numerous other buildings. The next day the Luftwaffe was back, destroying another 15 aircraft on the ground, finishing off the burning hangar and flattening a third. The Officers' Mess, Main Storeroom, Station Workshop, Hospital and the Chapel were all destroyed. Tragically a bomb shelter took a direct hit and collapsed, killing 13 and wounding 25 of those within it. It took days to put the fires out and weeks to repair the damage, but Tangmere was never put entirely out of action.

Soon after this the Germans gave up their efforts to gain control of the air preparatory to invading Britain and instead began to pound the cities as part of a longer term strategy to grind Britain to surrender. It did not work, of course, but the resulting blitz caused immense damage to the towns of Sussex as well as to London, Liverpool and other industrial cities.

The concrete blast walls beside the taxiway are a survivor of the jet age in the 1950s when Tangmere was a fighter base during the Cold War.

The beautiful stained-glass window in the small chapel at Aldingbourne's parish church devoted to those who served in the World War.

In 1941 Tangmere was taken over by Wing Commander Douglas Bader. Bader was a charismatic and daring fighter pilot who had his own ideas about taking the fight to the enemy. With five fighter squadrons under his command, Bader had a total of 60 Spitfires or Hurricanes always ready for combat, with others in reserve. With these he led daring raids into northern France, shooting up Luftwaffe airfields, strafing transport links and raiding any military target that could be found.

Bader and his men made life very difficult for the Germans. The aggressive sweeps hit a temporary setback when Bader was shot down in August 1941, but they soon began again. Thereafter Tangmere was used increasingly as a base for attacks on occupied territory. The programme reached a climax in 1944 with D-Day, by which time Sussex had a dozen other airfields.

After the war Tangmere remained a fighter base, but also played host to the high speed flight that set world records and to a secretive unit linked to the intelligence services. In 1967 the RAF moved out and the airfield was sold off.

4) After walking south about 100 yards the taxiway is blocked by a gate, the land beyond which is private. Turn left

The lane that leads from Aldingbourne to Oving is bordered by grass verges.

down a narrow footpath to exit the old airfield by way of a gate. This gives access to a lane. Walk along this lane to a T-junction and turn right to enter the village of Aldingbourne. As the road bends left the parish church is straight in front of you.

The distinctive octagonal spire of Oving church was a landmark used by pilots from Tangmere. It was an especially welcome sight for pilots returning safe from combat.

This St Mary's Church is usually open and is worth a visit. The oldest parts still standing date to around 1130, but the font is about three centuries older than that so there must have been a church here for at least 1200 years or so.

The south door has a cross carved on it that recalls a conflict much older than that fought out over RAF Tangmere, but one with very recent echoes. According to local tradition a man from Aldingbourne carved the downward stroke as he left the church to go on Crusade to fight the Moslems in the Holy Land in the late 12th century. Years later he returned to the village having fought his way to Jerusalem and prayed at the Church of the Holy Sepulchre. As he entered the Church for the first time

Oving churchyard has many ornately-carved tombstones.

since his return, the Crusader carved the horizontal bar to complete the cross that he had begun so many years earlier.

What was the Chapel of St George, built in 1190, was converted in 1946 to be a memorial to the men who served in the two world wars. There is a fine stained-glass window to the submarine officer Vice Admiral Sir Reginald Skelton, who died in 1956. As ever when visiting these rural churches you should make a donation to their upkeep.

5) Leave the church and continue along the lane to a T-junction with a second lane. Turn right.

6) This lane can be quite busy with traffic at times as it forms a handy side route for drivers trying to avoid rush hour jams on the A27, but there are pavements along some of its length and wide grass verges elsewhere.

7) Where the lane makes a sharp left bend just after entering the village of Oving turn right up Church Lane. On your left you will see St Andrew's Church.

The distinctive octagonal spire of this church was a well-known landmark for the pilots operating out of RAF Tangmere as they returned home from operations over France. The pilots would line up on the spire before turning to land on the runway. The first church built here was Norman, but the present structure is largely 13th century. There is much to see here but the church is best known for its magnificent stained-glass windows created by Powell & Sons to designs by William Morris. They alone make it worth stopping here a while.

8) Leave the church and turn left to walk past a row of almshouses. A turning on the left as Church Lane bends right will take you to the Gribble Inn, which serves hearty and well-cooked meals as well as offering a good range of beers. Otherwise, follow Church Lane round to the right to return to point 2 on the walk. Turn left to return along the track to the museum where the walk began.

One of the many exhibits that make the Tangmere Museum so worth a visit by anyone interested in aircraft.

The author enjoys a tasty cream tea at Jempson's in Battle, East Sussex.